THE REFERENCE SHELF (*Continued*)

Volume V. $3.00

No.

1. Prohibition: Modification of the Volstead Law. (Supplementary to Handbook) L. T. Beman.
   See also University Debaters' Annual, 1924-25. p. 321-66 and University Debaters' Annual, 1926-27. Ch. III.

2. Religious Teachings in the Public Schools. L. T. Beman.

E. IV. aters'

Mul-

's Annual, 1928-29. Ch. IV.

Volume VI. $4.80

No.

1. Financing of State Highways. J. E. Johnsen.

3. Baumes Law. J. E. Johnsen.

4. Thirteen-Month Calendar. J. E. Johnsen.
   See also University Debaters' Annual, 1929-30. Ch. VIII.

No.

5. Government Fund for Unemployment. H. M. Muller.

7. County Libraries. J. E. Johnsen.

8. County Manager Government. H. M. Muller.

9. Free Trade. J. E. Johnsen.

10. County Unit of School Administration. W. G. Carr.

Volume VII. $5.40

No.

2. Stability of Employment. J. E. Johnsen.

3. Lobbying in Congress. H. M. Muller.

4. Trends in University Education. J. G. Hodgson.

5. Conscription of Wealth in Time of War. J. E. Johnsen.

No.

6. Compulsory Unemployment Insurance. E. C. Buehler.

7. Chain Stores. Daniel Bloomfield.

8. The World Court. H. M. Muller.

9. Planning for Economic Stability. J. G. Hodgson.

10. Capitalism on Trial. J. E. Johnsen.

Volume VIII. $5.40

No.

2. State and Local Tax Revision. E. C. Buehler.

3. State and Local Tax Revision: Analytical Survey. E. C. Buehler.

4. Cancellation of International War Debts. J. G. Hodgson.

5. Debate Index. E. M. Phelps.

6. Federal Regulation of Banking; With Guaranty of Deposits. J. G. Hodgson.

No.

7. Stabilization of Money. J. G. Hodgson.

8. Chinese-Japanese War. J. E. Johnsen.

9. Federal Regulation of Motor Transport. H. M. Muller.

10. American vs. British System of Radio Control. E. C. Buehler.

THE REFERENCE SHELF (*Continued*)

Volume IX. $3.60

Volume X. $4.80

Volume XI. $6

Volume XII. $6

Future Issues to be Announced

The Reference Shelf is entered in the Readers' Guide to Periodical Literature, Education Index, Industrial Arts Index, Cumulative Book Index, and Book Review Digest.

PERIODICALS

containing articles not available in your local library can be had from our PERIODICALS DEPARTMENT at reasonable prices.

Ask for descriptive circular and prices.

THE H. W. WILSON COMPANY

950 University Avenue   New York City

THE REFERENCE SHELF

Vol. 11 No. 8

PEACE AND REARMAMENT

COMPILED BY
JULIA E. JOHNSEN

NEW YORK
THE H. W. WILSON COMPANY
1938

INTRODUCTORY NOTE

In the early part of 1938 a far-reaching departure was made from our customary policy in regard to national defense. The President asked of Congress a series of authorizations and appropriations for the largest naval and military program that we had ever found it essential to maintain in time of peace. Among the causes contributing to this situation were a series of conflicts abroad, brought about by aggressive policies of dictator nations in violation of the implications of international treaties and agreements, the new armament race initiated abroad and augmented by the expiration, on December 31, 1936, of the naval limitation agreements, and, finally the refusal of Japan to accede to the requests of Great Britain and the United States that she reveal her new naval construction program, thereby giving rise to serious apprehensions as to the Pacific area.

Much discussion has centered about the rearmament program thus inaugurated by the United States, its real necessity and aims, and, not least, its relation to the building up and maintenance of national and international peace. Apprehension has been widely manifest that a supernavy such as our defense program proposes, can only augur a foreign policy intended to interfere in the centers of conflict abroad. The feeling is strong that a moderate, traditional navy is alone consistent with our past ideals and our hopes of peace. At the other extreme, conviction has been likewise prevalent that until the world can be organized for a sound program of peace by international cooperation and enforcement of treaties, no advance in international comity can be made save by a show of such armed strength as will bring recalcitrant nations to terms.

The present number of the Reference Shelf is concerned particularly with recent discussions of rearmament and its relation to peace, with special stress upon the effects upon the world of armaments and our own defensive policy. In keeping with the policy of the Reference Shelf series, reprints and excerpts are presented to cover impartially varied points of view for the general reader and debater. A selected bibliography of recent material is included, classified so far as is possible according to the various view points. The accompanying summary of arguments is based on the underlying thought of armament strength adequate for forceful use in a lawless world if called for, as balanced against a moderate armament policy mainly or solely for home defense, supplemented by a major concern for the policies of a constructive program of peace.

JULIA E. JOHNSEN

July 25, 1938

CONTENTS

NEGATIVE DISCUSSION

SUMMARY OF ARGUMENTS

RESOLVED: *That a policy of rearmament is the best insurance for peace.*

INTRODUCTION

A. Definitions:
1. By "rearmament" is implied a definite increase in our national war establishment, with special emphasis on a strong navy.
   a. It implies more than replacement of obsolete units.
   b. It implies a navy greater than needed for purely defensive purposes.
   c. It implies, at the least, the approximate maintenance of the quantitative ratio of naval strength with the leading naval powers which are now engaged in naval increase.
2. By "insurance for peace" is implied relative strength in the realization of a lasting peace.
   a. It implies a predominant chance that we may avoid being drawn into a conflict.
   b. It implies the relative strength of the United States as an influence for peace elsewhere.

B. The question is important.
1. Aggressive acts and devastating wars have been entered upon in recent years by several nations.

2. Nations are rearming at an unprecedented rate.
3. Authorizations and appropriations have been made by this nation for the largest peace-time naval expansion program we have heretofore undertaken.
4. There has been much discussion as to whether the world armament programs in general, and our own contribution to armament expansion in particular, will contribute to a new world conflict or whether they are factors called for under present conditions for the maintenance of peace.

Affirmative

Rearmament is the best insurance for peace, for

I. In the present state of the world peace cannot be assured without the rearmament of the democratic nations.

   A. The peace of the world is being widely menaced.

      1. In recent years war has again shown a tendency to become widespread.

         a. Italy has carried on a war of conquest in Ethiopia.

         b. Japan has engaged in a series of conflicts in Manchuria and China.

         c. Germany forcibly took over Austria.

         d. Civil war in Spain has been given vital encouragement and support by other nations.

      2. Discontent and unrest are widely prevalent.

         a. Various nations have become dissatisfied with the status quo.

b. Ambitious nations are seeking the enhancement of their territorial and material interests.

c. Suspicion, distrust, fear and a sense of insecurity are prevalent.

3. The principles of international agreements and security are being undermined.

   a. International treaties and agreements are being ignored and violated with impunity.

   b. The League of Nations has been rendered impotent to deal with prevailing conditions.

4. Totalitarianism is widely threatening the principles of democracy.

   a. Dictatorships have suppressed democracy within their own countries.

   b. Aggressive policies of dictatorships are becoming a menace to other nations.

      (1) "Boring within" is being carried on in democratic states by fascist and Nazi elements.

      (2) A totalitarian alignment menaces the democratic nations of Europe and the world.

B. The lack of adequate defensive forces in a nation inclines to invite war.

1. The lack of potential strength places a nation at the mercy of strong and lawless states.

   a. Weakness is a direct incentive to attack.

      (1) Nations are ready to take advantage of others in proportion to their chances of success.

   (2) Opportunity may cause a nation
     to strike for material or tactical
     advantage.
  b. No adequate protective guarantee
   exists.
   (1) No effective international guar-
     antee is now operative.
   (2) Moral prohibition is notably
     weak if a nation chooses to
     ignore it.

2. The past immunity from attack of weak
 nations has been less due to their lack of
 defense than to other favoring factors.
  a. Time and occasion may have been
   inopportune.
  b. Other nations may have been watchful against a change in the balance of
   power.

3. Weak nations are relatively ineffective in
 the international policies that predispose
 to war or peace.
  a. They lack prestige to give weight to
   their views.
  b. They are at a diplomatic disadvantage
   as compared to states having more
   material strength.

4. History indicates that military weakness
 has in many cases been a factor in the
 initiation of war.
  a. The weakness of Manchuria, Ethiopia,
   Austria and China were factors in
   their late invasions.
  b. The weakness of Belgium was an
   incentive to its attack in 1914.
  c. If we had been strong in our national
   defenses in the initial period of the

World war it is less likely we should have been drawn in.

   (1) The nations would have been more circumspect in over-riding our rights.

   (2) If our strength had been sufficient and our willingness to defend international principles by force of arms if necessary had been undoubted, it is possible the war might never have occurred.

C. Sole reliance on the power of peaceful policies is unwise at the present time.

  1. Disarmament is at the moment an impracticable ideal.

    a. Arms limitation has failed under past agreements.

      (1) It failed to accomplish more than relative limitation.

      (2) Since the expiration of naval treaties it has been largely abandoned.

      (3) Rearmament is now widespread.

        (a) Totalitarian nations are rearming in order to capitalize their new opportunities now that they are unchecked.

        (b) Other nations must increase their strength proportionately to guard against menaces.

    b. Nations cannot disarm alone.

  2. Other efforts to establish a workable peace have been inadequate.

    a.   The League of Nations has been in-
effective in many vital policies.

      (1) We ourselves have failed to give
it adequate support.

      (2) The Great Powers have mis-
used it.

        (a) They have used it for poli-
tical ends.

        (b) They have used it for the
maintenance of the status
quo instead of as an instrument for equality and
justice among the nations.

    b.   No other adequate instrument for
international cooperation in peace has
been instituted.

3.   Measures considered as national policies
against warring nations are largely unworkable and unwise.

    a.   Isolation and neutrality policies are
largely unworkable.

      (1) They are difficult of consistent
application.

      (2) Other nations neutralize their
effects.

    b.   Isolation and neutrality are largely
selfish and detrimental in effect.

      (1) They are largely a hands-off
policy.

      (2) They ignore fundamental
wrongs and our obligation
toward them.

      (3) They may definitely aid ag-
gressor nations.

        (a) The withdrawal of con-
cern which they imply

may give encouragement in the pursuit of their lawless course.

(b) Aggressor nations are normally stronger and more resourceful than their victims.

D. A strong rearmament policy would not necessarily lead to war.

1. Strong armaments do not necessarily lead to aggressive policies.

a. Armaments do not necessarily incline to provocative policies.

b. Aggression is no longer a likely motive for democratically inclined nations.

2. Wars are due to a multitude of causes.

a. Economic and other maladjustments are factors conductive to war.

b. Nationalistic interests may require defense against encroachments.

c. Principles and the protection of world order may require arms support.

3. It is not likely militarism within a nation would arise by reason of rearmament alone.

II. Our rearmament program would best conduce to the preservation of our peace in view of world conditions.

A. Altho protected by our geographical position and other favoring factors there is no reason to assume we may be immune from the menace of a possible war.

1. Recent events abroad have shown there is no real certainty of immunity from provocation by lawless nations.

2.   Natural protectiveness afforded by distance has greatly lessened.

   a.   Political and economic isolation are impossible in the modern world.

   b.   Airplanes and modern warfare have greatly lessened the value of geographical protectiveness.

3.   Incidents may arise in the protection of our vital interests to draw us into war.

   a.   Our rights, protection of citizens abroad, commerce, and similar interests may give rise to conflict.

   b.   Our national honor may be at stake.

   c.   It may be necessary to uphold the principles of liberty and democracy against those nations which would submerge them.

      (1) It would be a moral obligation.

      (2) Not to do so might bring the same menace home to us.

4.   It is not beyond possibility that a menace might arise close to our own shores.

   a.   Conditions in the Western hemisphere might call for our vital concern.

      (1) The Monroe Doctrine might be threatened by a foreign aggressor.

      (2) The Panama Canal might be menaced.

      (3) The lodgement of a foreign power on outlying possessions or contiguous territory might constitute a menace.

         (a) Japan might become established in Lower California or the Aleutian Islands.

        (b) A foreign power might acquire or take possession of some island or territory representing a strategetical menace.

    b. An enemy might gain strategetical advantage by working within.

    c. A coalition of aggressor nations might menace us.

B. A supernavy as projected in our expansion program would be an advantage if war should come.

    1. It would guard against delays that might prove a serious handicap.

        a. It takes time to create an effective navy.

            (1) Large battleships take at least three years to build.

            (2) It takes time to train personnel.

        b. It would enable us to strike promptly and effectively.

    2. It would tend to minimize the duration and losses of war.

        a. It would minimize economic losses.

        b. It would minimize loss of life.

    3. It would contribute to the more effective protection of our home territory.

        a. We could better prevent menace to our coasts.

        b. If necessary we could protect both coasts at once.

    4. A supernavy would give us the advantage of carrying war far beyond our borders.

        a. It would enable us to keep an enemy far from our shores.

        b. It would enable us to maintain distant bases of operation.

   c. We could better protect our com-
     merce from being driven off the seas
     and keep open our lines of supply.
   d. We could more effectively guard our
     outlying possessions.
     (1) We could more adequately pro-
       tect Alaska, the Hawaiian
       Islands, Guam, Samoa, Panama
       Canal Zone, Puerto Rico, the
       Virgin Islands.
     (2) We could better protect the
       Philippines until their complete
       independence is proclaimed.
  5. A supernavy would enable us to join more
    effectively in collective action if called for.
 C. Our armaments would not constitute danger.
  1. They are intended to protect our own
    interests, not for aggression.
  2. Our fully expanded program would not
    profoundly alter the relative strength of
    navies.
   a. Our expanded program would not be
     effective for two or more years.
   b. Other navies are expanding at the
     same or greater rate.
   c. It is possible that before it is fully
     realized the nations may enter upon
     another limitation agreement.
  3. They would not be a danger to ourselves.
   a. They would not lead to militarism.
   b. Public opinion would prevent abuses.

III. Rearmament would best promote the ultimate interests of world security and lasting peace.
  A. At the present time armament strength would
    maintain the enforcement of world order.

1. Until international morality and cooperation are more securely established there is no substitute for potential power.
   a. Superior force is the only policy dictatorship countries will heed.
   b. Potential strength alone will give confidence in upholding principles.
2. Respect for the rights of nations must be made an international policy in the interests of common security.
   a. The abandonment of principles of law and order to the chaotic and lawless forces menacing the world today would jeopardize our own security.
   b. The abandonment of those principles would make us recreant to our moral duty in the international order.
   c. If agreements voluntarily adopted are evaded or violated at will there can be no assurance of a stable society.
3. Potential strength would aid in mitigating undue violation of treaties.
   a. The presence of potential coercive force which may be used if conditions properly call for them is a deterrent.
   b. It would not assume unlawful coercion, but merely that understandings voluntarily entered upon among nations be upheld against disruptive forces for the protection and good of all.
4. Our own armament strength would be an asset in improving conditions of world order.

    a. Other countries are handicapped in dealing with violators of international order alone.

        (1) Individually other countries are for the most part too weak.

        (2) Agreements between countries for collective action are difficult.

            (a) Political entanglements handicap them.

            (b) Violators are too strong and are supported by other countries which hope to gain similar advantages.

            (c) The uncertainty of the policy we may follow prevents agreements.

    b. We are in a better position to take the initiative.

        (1) We hold a strong material position.

        (2) Our moral leadership is a factor of weight.

            (a) We are generally devoted to principle.

            (b) We are reasonably detached from self-interest.

        (3) We are predominantly peace-loving.

B. The backing of a strong armament program can best influence the attainment of constructive measures of peace.

    1. It would give us enhanced prestige and weight in diplomacy and the councils of the world.

   a.   Unpreparedness in the face of world needs tends to the belittling of our counsels.

   b.   Preparedness adds realism.

2.   It would tend to eventually promote a real disarmament.

   a.   The economic burden of armaments will lead to their own cure.

   b.   Our rivalry in armaments will the sooner tend to check them.

      (1) We can outdistance any other nations.

      (2) As the strongest nation we can most effectively bargain for the limitation of arms.

3.   Such a program would aid in promoting other constructive measures of peace.

   a.   It would make nations more amenable to influence designed to strengthen peace.

      (1) It would give nations more confidence in the realization of real security.

      (2) It would provide a buffer until it is attained.

   b.   It would strengthen international co-operation.

   c.   It would tend to strengthen world organization.

      (1) It would tend to give effectiveness to the League of Nations or provide some substitute for it.

      (2) It would encourage other constructive efforts for a workable peace.

   d.   It would tend to encourage collective action for peace.

NEGATIVE

Rearmament would not best insure peace, for

I. The tendency of expanded armaments is to provoke war.

    A. Armament increases inevitably lead to the vicious circle of armament races among the nations.

        1. Fear and suspicion leads each country to vie with others in feverish building.

            a. Each wishes for its safety to avoid being caught unprepared.

            b. Each wishes adequate armament for all contingencies of defense.

            c. Each wishes to maintain its relative ratio of armament with neighboring nations or leading powers.

        2. The armament race so initiated is intensified by unconscious or deliberate aggravation.

            a. The public press and public discussions contribute to apprehensiveness.

            b. Deliberate propaganda may be set in motion to intensify fear.

            c. Munitions vendors and others financially interested in armaments take advantage of any situation to promote larger sales.

                (1) They recognize no nationalism, but sell to any country that will buy.

                (2) A war means to them a greater opportunity for business.

            d. Other interests that would profit thru war become active.

3. The strained relations which arise from such situations are readily provocative of war.
   a. Incidents are magnified.
   b. Misundersanding may cause precipitate mobilization and action.
   c. A spark may cause an explosion.

B. Large armaments are contributory to wars in other ways.
1. They contribute to the intensification of attitudes that may lead to war.
   a. They intensify the nationalistic spirit.
      (1) National "rights" and interests become issues.
      (2) Statesmen become unduly sensitive to "national honor."
   b. Militarism is encouraged.
      (1) Military men rattle sabres.
      (2) People become fired to the "glory of war."
   c. National ambition, arrogance and power are intensified.
2. Large armaments are strongly contributory to aggressive wars.
   a. They provide means to carry on war.
      (1) Without strong armaments they would not risk it.
   b. They provide incentives for war.
      (1) Armaments make for aggressive policies.
      (2) A nation may precipitate a war before its rivals become strong.
   c. History indicates that wars have repeatedly been precipitated by reason of the preparedness of nations responsible for them.

        (1) Germany's preparedness was a leading factor in the origination of the World war.

        (2) The military strength of Japan was directly responsible for her encroachments in Manchuria and China.

        (3) Italy's strength was an incentive to her attack on Ethiopia.

        (4) Germany's secret rearming was responsible for her invasion of Austria.

   3. Secret diplomacy and military alliances are encouraged by armaments.

      a. These give less tendency to be conciliating.

      b. They may lead to "incidents."

   4. The principle of armaments in international policy is that of diplomatic coercion and is apt to bring a return in kind.

II. Our rearmament program is not conducive to the preservation of our peace.

   A. It is needless for self defense.

      1. Our geographical position protects us.

        a. We are isolated from likely fields of conflicts.

          (1) It is unlikely there would be any serious menace from the North or South.

          (2) We are protected on the east and west by an expanse of ocean.

        b. No enemy could conceivably transport across either ocean a fleet of sufficient size to seriously menace us.

(1) It would require a navy larger than any nation now possesses.

(2) It would require auxiliary fleets for its support larger than any nation now possesses.

(3) No likely enemy has adequate bases near us.

c. An undertaking of such magnitude as would be required to wage war on our shores would seriously weaken any nation that might undertake it.

(1) The support of such a war would deplete their resources.

(2) It would leave them exposed to enemies nearer home.

2. It is hardly conceivable that any nation would attack us.

a. There would be little motive for aggressive attack.

3. In case an attack should come we could quickly enter upon effective measures of defense.

a. Our navy is adequate to protect our coasts.

(1) It can be used in either ocean.

(2) Its activity would be reinforced by coast defenses and action of the army air forces.

b. We could quickly strengthen our defenses in many ways.

(1) Industrial mobilization would lead to the rapid procurement of materials.

(2) Our nucleus of defense could be rapidly expanded in other ways.

C. There is no real security in armaments.
1. The safety they guarantee to one nation is a source of fear to another.
2. Preparedness may not prevent war.
3. The relative strength of defensive establishments of the nations is likely to remain approximately the same.
    a. The increase in one nation is matched or surpassed by others.
    b. They differ mainly in kind and a nation's ability to finance them.
4. The waste entailed by armaments is a distinct drain upon real security.
    a. They are unproductive.
    b. Many instruments of military and naval warfare become obsolete in a few years and must be replaced.
    c. The financial cost to the nation is heavy.
        (1) It places upon it an intolerable tax burden.
        (2) It may lead to danger of financial collapse.
    d. In case of eventual real war the national reserves are sooner exhausted.
B. Superarmament has no legitimate place in our national policy.
1. It can only be intended for action elsewhere.
    a. It is larger than is needed for our own territory and adjacent waters.
    b. It is a step toward any distant action we may enter upon.
        (1) It would be an incentive to protect private interests and citizens in war zones and elsewhere.

        (2) It would be an incentive for concerted action with Great Britain.

        (3 It would be an incentive for policing the whole world and the enforcing of orderly processes everywhere.

2. There is no valid reason for the use of our armed forces in other lands.

    a. The protection of distant territory and interests are not worth going to war over.

        (1) Our economic interests are not worth the greater economic cost of a conflict.

        (2) It is doubtful if they would be worth the sacrifice of human lives.

    b. There is no reason why we should defend the Philippines.

        (1) They are destined for independence and are no longer our concern.

        (2) They could in any case be taken over by a first class power such as Japan, if she was determined to take them.

    c. We are not called upon to police the world.

        (1) It is not our legitimate concern.

        (2) It is not to our own interest.

3. Such a superarmament policy might lead to conditions at home detrimental to our well being.

    a. It would tend to break down resistance to war.

          (1) It would tend to educate people for war.

          (2) It would promote the militarism that might instigate it.

    b. It would be financially detrimental.

          (1) It is an enormous expense.

          (2) It deprives the country of appropriations for other urgently needed projects.

          (3) The programs projected to not remove profits from war.

              (a) The cost of building capital ships has risen from over \$60,000,000 for those being built to over \$70,000,000 for projected ones.

              (b) Destroyers built for \$1,000,000 during the war are now costing \$5,000,000.

              (b) The projected industrial mobilization program would not prevent undue profiteering.

    c. It might conceivably lead to a military dictatorship.

C. Superarmament would not in itself prevent our being involved in war.

    1. Rearmament could in itself furnish no safeguard against our entry upon war if conditions otherwise called for it.

        a. It could furnish no safeguard against aggressive action on our part.

        b. It could furnish no assurance against hasty action or abuse.

2. The contention that strong armament might prevent wars arising elsewhere is overdrawn.

    a. Nations are moved by conditions and interests of their own.

    b. A "big stick" policy might very likely lead to resentment and cause rather than prevent conflict.

III. World peace can best be attained without undue armament.

A. Peace policies are not at fault for the failure to realize world security.

    1. World insecurity is in large part due to unsettled international problems.

        a. World-wide economic maladjustments have contributed to it.

        b. International injustices have contributed to it.

    2. The peace program is fundamentally sound.

        a. It is based on the right principles.

        b. Its shortcomings are due to the lack of sufficiently wide application.

    3. The past attempt in the limitation of armaments was a gain for peace rather than a failure.

        a. It was a strong force for peace while it was operative.

B. The maintenance of the war program at the minimum required for national needs would strengthen efforts for peace.

    1. It would strengthen the moral forces for peace.

        a. It would remove inconsistencies inherent in such a program.

       b.   It would tend to minimize forces opposing such effort.

       c.   It would inspire greater confidence on the part of other nations.

  2. It would strengthen the constructive program for peace.

       a.   Greater support would be forthcoming.

         (1) From the public.

         (2) Substantial government support might be forthcoming.

       b.   The support of the peace program even to a portion of the extent given to our war establishment would be an immense force.

C. The attainment of world peace lies in the strengthening of all peace channels.

  1. The reinforcing of existing channels for international cooperation would materially help the realization of lasting peace.

       a.   There is need for increased conferences with other nations.

       b.   International economic cooperation is called for.

       c.   The strengthening of and cooperation with the League of Nations is greatly needed.

  2. Provision should be made for new channels as called for by changing conditions.

       a.   Means are called for to deal effectively with causes of discontent and international injustice.

       b.   It is essential to provide a channel or channels for the enforcement of international agreements, in the interests of world order.

BIBLIOGRAPHY

An asterisk (*) preceding a reference indicates that the article or a part of it has been reprinted in this volume.

BIBLIOGRAPHIES

Atkinson, Henry A. Prelude to peace. p. 211-16. Harper & Bros. N.Y. '37.

Carnegie Endowment for International Peace. Library. Peace forces of today; select list of recent books and articles on various aspects of the peace movement, with annotations. Mary Alice Matthews, comp. 54p. (Reading list no. 27). The Endowment. 700 Jackson Pl. Wash., D.C. My. 20, '38.

Engelbrecht, H. C. Notes and references. *In* his Revolt against war. p. 337-53. Dodd, Mead & Co. N.Y. '37.

Hartley, Livingston. Is America afraid? sources. p. 450-3. Prentice-Hall. N.Y. '37.

Johnson, Julia E. comp. Selected articles on national defense: bibliography. p. xxxix-lxxxiii. H. W. Wilson Co. N.Y. '28.

Phelps, Edith M. ed. Armed intervention for protection of American interests abroad: bibliography. *In* University Debaters' Annual, 1933-1934. p. 97-103. H. W. Wilson Co. N.Y.'34.

Phelps, Edith M. ed. War the highest form of patriotism: bibliography. *In* University Debaters' Annual 1934-1935. p. 403-8. H. W. Wilson Co. N.Y. '35.

Schnapper, M. B. Youth faces war and fascism: an annotated bibliography. 18p. mimeo. National Youth Committee. American League Against War and Fascism. 268 4th Av. N.Y. '37.

General References
Books, Pamphlets and Documents

Background of war. By the editors of Fortune. 296p. Alfred A. Knopf. N.Y. '37.

Reprints articles appearing in Fortune. 15:97-103+. Mr.; 81-8+. Ap.; 95-101+. My.; 82-91+. Je.; 16:68-78+. Jl.; 70-7+. Ag. '37.

Baldwin, Hanson W. The caissons roll; a military survey of Europe. 323p. Alfred A. Knopf. N.Y. '38.

Beard, Charles A. Navy: defense or portent? 198p. Harper & Bros. N.Y. '32.

Brunauer, Esther Caukin, ed. National defense. 51p. Womans Press. N.Y. '37.

Call, Arthur Deerin. Three views of collective security. 18p. mimeo. Institute of Public Affairs, Univ. of Virginia. Charlottesville, Va. Jl. 5, '37.

Cripps, Stafford. Struggle for peace. 287p. Victor Gollancz. Lond. '36.

Cronbach, Abraham. Quest for peace. 223p. Sinai Press. Cincinnati. '37.

Denlinger, Sutherland & Gary, Charles B. War in the Pacific; a study of navies, peoples and battle problems. 338p. Robert M. McBride & Co. N.Y. '36.

Dulles, Foster Rhea. America in the Pacific; a century of expansion. 299p. Houghton Mifflin Co. N.Y. '38.

Dupuy, Richard Ernest & Eliot, George Fielding. If war comes. 368p. Macmillan Co. N.Y. '37.

Eagleton, Clyde. Analysis of the problem of war. 132p. Ronald Press. N.Y. '37.

Edmonds, James E. Fighting fools. 373p. D. Appleton-Century Co. N.Y. '38.

Geneva Institute of International Relations. Problems of peace: League and the future of the collective system. 254p. George Allen & Unwin. Lond. '37.

Hagood, Johnson. We can defend America. 321p. Doubleday, Doran & Co. N.Y. '37.

Heald, Stephen & Wheeler-Bennett, John W. eds. Documents on international affairs, 1936. Oxford Univ. Press. N.Y. '37.

Address of August 14, 1936 by Franklin D. Roosevelt, and of September 15, 1936 by Cordell Hull.

Healy, Thomas H. Handbook of national defense and peace. 336p. Ransdell Inc. Wash. D.C. '36.

Herring, Hubert. And so to war. 178p. Yale Univ. Press. New Haven. '38.

Hinton, Harold B. America gropes for peace. 214p. Johnson Pub. Co. N.Y.'38.

Hirst, Francis W. Armaments; the race and the crisis. 171p. Cobden-Sanderson. Lond. '37.

Howe, Quincy. England expects every American to do his duty. 238p. Simon & Schuster. N.Y. '37.

Institute of International Affairs. Proceedings. 14:161-4. '36. Is anything more important than peace? Clyde Eagleton.

Institute of World Affairs. Proceedings, 1936. p. 89-94, 119-25, 161-205. Univ. of Southern California. Los Angeles. '37.

Ishimaru, Tota. Next world war. tr. by B. Matsukawa. 352p. Hurst & Blackett. Lond. '37.

Liddell Hart, Basil Henry. Europe in arms. 287p. Random House. N.Y. '37.

Liepmann, Heinz. Death from the skies. 286p. Martin Secker & Warburg. Lond. '37.

Madariaga, Salvador de. World's design. 291p. George Allen & Unwin. Lond. '38.

Millis, Walter. Future of sea power in the Pacific. 51p. (World Affairs Par. No. 9) Foreign Policy Assn. 8 W. 40th St. N.Y. '35.

Millis, Walter. Road to war: America 1914-1917. 466p. Houghton Mifflin Co. Bost. '35.

National Education Association. Proceedings. 1937: 128-34. Present situation facing the United States in regard to the possibility of war. Raymond Leslie Buell.

Peace programs. 55p. mimeo. Department of Synagogue and School Extension. Merchants Bldg. Cincinnati, O. n.d.

Phelps, Edith M. ed. Japan and naval parity. *In* University Debaters' Annual, 1934-1935. p. 409-50. H. W. Wilson Co. N.Y. '35.
Bibliography, p. 445-50.

Potter, Pitman B. Collective security and peaceful change. 38p. (Public Policy Pam. no. 24) Univ. of Chicago Press. Chic. '37.
Suggested readings, p. 37-8.

Pratt, Fletcher. Navy, a history: the story of a service in action. 496p. Doubleday, Doran & Co. N.Y. '38.

Raushenbush, H. Stephen & Raushenbush, Joan. The final choice; America between Europe and Asia. 331p. John Day. N.Y. '37.

Richmond, Herbert. Navy. 128p. William Hodge & Co. Lond. '37.

Roosevelt, Eleanor. This troubled world. 47p. H. C. Kinsey & Co. N.Y. '38.

Russell, Bertrand. Why nations love war. *In his* Justice in war time. p. 58-64. Open Court Pub. Co. Chicago. '17.

Stone, William T. America: a nation in arms? *In* Quigley, Harold S. Peace or war? a conference. p. 150-61. (Day and Hour ser. no. 17 & 18) Univ. of Minnesota Press. Minneapolis. Je. '37.

Stone, William T. & Eichelberger, Clark M. Peaceful change the alternative to war. 46p. (Headline Books no. 12) Foreign Policy Assn. 8 W. 40th St. N.Y. '37.

Stone, William T. & Goslin, Ryllis Alexander. Billions for defense. 46p. (Headline Books no. 9) Foreign Policy Assn. 8 W. 40th St. N.Y. '37.

Tansill, Charles Callan. America goes to war. 731p. Little, Brown & Co. Bost. '38.

Tobenkin, Elias. Peoples want peace. 244p. G. P. Putnam's Sons. N.Y. '38.

Toynbee, A. J. & Boulter, V. M. Survey of international affairs, 1936. p. 117-60. Oxford Univ. Press. N.Y. '37.

United States. House. Committee on Naval Affairs. To establish the composition of the United States navy; hearings January 31-February 28, 1938 on H.R. 9218. 1937-2889p. (no. 620) (75th Cong. 3d sess.) Supt. of Doc. Wash. D.C. '38.

United States. Senate. Committee on Naval Affairs. Naval expansion program; hearings on H.R. 9218, April 4-13, 1938. 65th Cong. 3d sess. Supt. of Doc. Wash. D.C. '38.

United States. War Department. Annual report of the Secretary of War to the President, 1937. 99p. Govt. Ptg. Off. Wash. D.C. '37.

Vagts, Alfred. History of militarism. 510p. W. W. Norton & Co. N.Y. '37.

Wright, Louise Leonard. Toward a collective peace system. 58p. National League of Women Voters. 726 Jackson Pd. Wash. D.C. '37(?)

PERIODICALS

Amerasia. 1:5-8. Mr. '37. Has America a naval policy? Chester H. Rowell.

*Amerasia. 2:63-7. Mr. '38. Navy as an instrument of diplomacy. William T. Stone.

American Journal of International Law. 31:688-93. O. '37. Secretary of State Hull's pillars of enduring peace. George A. Finch.

American Mercury. 40:21-5. Ja. '37. Japan's secret navy. Fletcher Oratt.

American Mercury. 41:6-18. My. '37. Red road to war. Harold Lord Varney.

American Review. 9:433-55. O. '37. China and the Geneva system. Douglas Jerrold.
Same. Nineteenth Century. 122:385-401. O. '37.
America's Town Meeting of the Air. Bulletin. 3:5-32. F. 14, '38. Should Congress adopt the President's armament proposals? Maury Maverick, Edouard V. Iztac and Russell Cartright Stroup.
America's Town Meeting of the Air. Bulletin. 3:5-30. Ap. 11, '38. Is there a way to world peace? Anne O'Hare McCormick and others.
Annals of the American Academy. 192:42-50. Jl. '37. United States in a war minded world. Carroll Binder.
Asia. 37:409-13. Je. '37. More American air bases. John Williams.
Asia. 37:716-19. O. '37. Arms race in Asia. William Henry Chamberlin.
Atlantic Monthly. 161:492-4. Ap. '38. War and peace, a reality. R. De Roussy de Sales.
Barron's. 17:11. Mr. 22, '37. Looking beyond rearmament to inevitable unsettlement and economic collapse. Marcus Nadler.
Christian Century. 53:526-8. Ap. 8, '36. War is not inevitable!
Christian Century. 54:175-7. F. 10, '37. Millions for defense?
Christian Century. 54:413-16. Mr. 31, '37. 1917—then and now—1937. Kirby Page.
Christian Century. 54:1127-9. S. 15, '37. Shattered fabric of world peace.
Christian Century. 54:1285-8. O. 20, '37. Crisis in American peace policy.
Christian Century. 55:38-40. Ja. 12, '38. Where is Mr. Roosevelt heading?
Christian Century. 55:230-1. F. 23, '38. Why Mr. Roosevelt wants a super-navy.
Christian Century. 55:234-7. F. 23, '38. How America entered the next war. John Haynes Holmes.

Christian Century. 55:458-61. Ap. 13, '38. A fire sale on sanity? Taylor Merrill.

Christian Science Monitor Weekly Magazine Section. p. 1-2+. Ja. 6, '37. Shall the United States withdraw from the far Pacific? William C. Rivers; Dudley W. Knox.

Christian Science Monitor Weekly Magazine Section. p. 1-2+. Mr. 9, '38. How many ships make security? James Phinney Baxter; Ships, or planes, or naval pacts? symposium of opinion.

Christian Science Monitor Weekly Magazine Section. p. 1-2+. My. 18, '38. How can United States serve peace. Frederick J. Libby; Clark M. Eichelberger.

Commercial and Financial Chronicle. 146:650-2. Ja. 29, '38. United States and world armament.

Commercial and Financial Chronicle. 146:1158-9. F. 19, '38. Japanese note to United States, Great Britain and France refuses to give naval building data.

Commonweal. 27:449-50. F. 18, '38. Mobilization for chaos.

*Commonweal. 28:93-5. My. 20, '38. Isolation, cooperation and peace. Elizabeth M. Lynsky.

Congressional Digest. 13:97-122. Ap. '34. America and the national defense problem.

Congressional Digest. 16:101-28. Ap. '37. Proposed nationalization of munitions.

Congressional Digest. 17:67-96. Mr. '38. Roosevelt's national defense program.

Congressional Record. 83: (current) 1585-6. Ja. 28, '38. Message to Congress. Franklin D. Roosevelt.

Congressional Record. 83: (current) 7392-400, 7406-13. Ap. 21, '38. Naval expansion program; debate.

Congressional Record. 83: (current) 7718-48. Ap. 27, '38. Naval expansion problem: debate.

Congressional Record. 83: (current) 7812-34, 7921-42. Ap. 28, 29, '38. Naval expansion problem: debate.

*Congressional Record. 83: (current) 10761-4. Je. 3, '38. Spirit of international law. Cordell Hull.

Contemporary Review. 149:668-77. Je. '36. Armaments race. W. Arnold-Forster.

Current History. 45:35-46. Ja. '37. Peace on earth.

Current History. 45:25-34. F. '37. National lifelines.

Current History. 46:27. Ag. '37. Enter armaments.

Current History. 48:13-14. Mr. '38. Armaments for peace.

Current History. 48:14. Ap. '38. War mania.

Current History. 48:31-4. Ap. '38. Our fourth-estate looks at the navy. Burt M. McConnell.

Current History. 48:18-20. My. '38. Mr. Roosevelt's little navy. John C. Winslow.

Digest. 1:26. O. 16, '37. Armaments and peace. Guglielmo Ferrero.

Dynamic America. 6:10-15. Mr. '38. Shout the war lords down! Harry W. Pascoe.

Economist (London). 126:449-50. F. 27, '37. Peace— and plenty of arms.

Editorial Research Reports. p. 71-86. Jl. 24, '37. New race in armaments. Buel W. Patch.

English Review. 64:529-43. My. '37. Future warfare. Liddell Hart.

Food for Forums. p.1-36. My. '38. American foreign policy and the big navy question.

Foreign Affairs. 15:235-53. Ja. '37. Armies of Europe. Liddell Hart.

Foreign Affairs. 15:484-94. Ap. '37. Naval bases in the Pacific. William Henry Chamberlin.

Foreign Affairs. 15:729-44. Jl. '37. Supervising the American traffic in arms. Joseph C. Green.

Foreign Affairs. 16:388-400. Ap. '38. Alternative American policies in the Far East. Tyler Dennett.

Foreign Affairs. 16:430-44. Ap. '38. America rearms. Hanson W. Baldwin.

Foreign Policy Reports. 12:282-92. F. 15, '37. Rising tide of armament. William T. Stone and Helen Fisher.

Foreign Policy Reports. 13:18-29. Ap. 1, '37. Can war profits be eliminated? Harold Tobin and R. L. Buell.

Fortnightly Review. 149 (n.s.143):129-36. F. '38. Rule of fear; ineffective methods of attaining peace. Guglielmo Ferrero.

Same. International Conciliation. 339:139-55. Ap. '38.

Fortune. 12:38-49+. S. '35. Who's in the army now?

Fortune. 17:55-65+. Mr. '38. Big navy.

Forum. 97:89-95, 165-70, 249-54. F.-Ap. '37. How to stay out of war.

*Forum. 98:49-53. Ag. '37. Keeping out of war. Henry Goddard Leach.

Forum. 98:223-7. N. '37. Triumph of lawlessness. Norman Angell.

Harper's Magazine. 176:337-48. Mr. '38. We lose the next war. Elmer Davis.

Harper's Magazine. 176:652-64. My. '38. Where are you going, Mr. President? trend of our foreign policy. Hubert Herring.

Harper's Magazine. 176:511-19. Jl. '38. Italy's over-estimated power. George Fielding Eliot.

Information Service. 16:1-2. Mr. 6, '37. Rising tide of rearmament.

International Conciliation. 340:193-209. My. '36. If war comes, what will America's policy be? George S. Montgomery, Jr.

International Conciliation. 341:278-91. Je. '38. Our national defenses. George Norlin.

Ladies' Home Journal. 54:12. Jl. '37. Dilemma of a pacifist. Dorothy Thompson.

Literary Digest. 123:5-6. Ja. 9, '37. Naval race.

Literary Digest. 125:3-5. F. 12, '38. New strength for navy.

Living Age. 351:382-3. Ja. '37. World expenditures for armament.

Nation. 146:376-8, 403-5, 435-6. Ap. 2-16, '38. How to keep out of war; peace-poll returns.

Nation. 146:407-10. Ap. 9, '38. America's gift to aggressors. H. C. Engelbrecht.

National City Bank of New York. Economic conditions. p. 41-3. Mr. '37.

New Republic. 90:293-4. Ap. 14, '37. Perils of peace.

New Republic. 91:209-10, 224. Je. 30, '37. Can America ensure peace? Will America stop another war? J. A. Hobson.

New Republic. 93:253-4. Ja. 5, '38. Will we arm to scare Japan?

New Republic. 94:32-3. F. 16, '38. What is the navy for?

New Republic. 94:210. Mr. 30, '38. Rough seas for the super-navy. Charles A. Beard.

New Republic. 94, Pt. 2:233-58. Mr. 30, '38. National defense, a progressive policy; symposium.
  *For impregnable defense. George Fielding Eliot. p. 240-9.

New Republic. 95:21-2. My. 11, '38. Aleutians and national defense. William C. Rivers; George Fielding Eliot.

New Statesman and Nation. n.s. 13:802-4. My. 15, '37. What is happening in the peace movement? C. E. M. Joad.

New York Herald Tribune. p. 23. S. 11, '36. Peace by will power. Dorothy Thompson.

*New York Times. p. 1, 16. O. 6, '37. Text of President Roosevelt's anti-war address at Chicago.
  Same. Vital Speeches. 4:2-4. O. 15, '37.

New York Times. p. 4. Ja. 16, '38. Program for peace: radio speech to the Women's National Republican Club. Herbert Hoover.

New York Times. Sec. 4. p. 8. Ja. 30, '38. Once more we decide to have naval parity. Edwin L. James.

New York Times Magazine. p. 4, 17. Je. 20, '37. When the "next war" breaks on the world. Hanson W. Baldwin.

New York Times Magazine. p. 11, 17. Jl. 25, '37. Errors of the left in the right-left war. Salvador de Madariaga.

New York Times Magazine. p. 1-2+. N. 28, '37. Boom days for the merchant of arms. Hanson W. Baldwin.

New York Times Magazine. p. 1-2, 27. F. 20, '38. Nation weighs its world policies. Harold B. Hinton.

New York Times Magazine. p. 4-5+. Jc. 26, '38. Spy flourishes in an era of rearmament. Hanson W. Baldwin.

Newsweek. 11:11-12. F. 7, '38. Our duty, a navy second to none.

Newsweek. 11:9-10. F. 21, '38. Navy race: Japan passes the buck to Mr. Roosevelt.

North American Review. 245, no. 2:240-55. (Je) '38. Have we bonds with the British? Quincy Howe.

Pacific Affairs. 11:208-23. Je. '38. Armed strength of the United States in the Pacific. Alexander Kirafly.

Political Quarterly. 8:21-35. Ja. '37. Arms and peace. Leonard Woolf.

Political Science Quarterly. 53:1-13. Mr. '38. American military policy and the national security. Edward Mead Earle.

Political Science Quarterly. 53:173-85. Je. '38. Must it be war with Japan? Paul T. Homan.

Popular Science Monthly. 132:26-7+. Ja. '38. How good are the new war machines? Arthur Grahame.

Review of Reviews. 95:76-7. Mr. '37. Prospects of war. A. C. Temperley.

Review of Reviews. 96:34-5+. Jl. '37. M-day in America. Frank C. Hanighen.

Round Table. 27:772-7. S. '37. Booms, slumps and armaments.

Round Table. 28:1-18. D. '37. Power and opinion in world affairs.

Round Table. 28:297-306. Mr. '38. Warp and woof of American policy.

Saturday Evening Post. 209:12-13+. Ap. 10, '37. Airplanes can't sink battleships. Jack Lincke.

Saturday Evening Post. 210:5+. N. 27, '37. This peace is a cheat. John Gunther.

Saturday Evening Post. 210:8-9+. Mr. 5, '38. Peace, inc.; peace movement in the United States. Stanley High.

Scholastic. 31:11-12. N. 6, '37. Price of peace. Lincoln Steffens.

Scholastic. 31:25S-27S. N. 6, '37. How much are the nations of the world spending for armaments?

Scholastic. 32:15S. F. 5, '38. President pushes big navy construction program.

Scholastic. 32:15S. F. 26, '38. World navy race is on.

Scientific American. 157:206-7. O. '37. Peace-time preparedness. J. G. Harbord.

Scientific American. 159:9-11. Jl. '38. Air-minded first line of defense. Jonas H. Ingram.

Sociology and Social Research. 22:239-45. Ja. '38. Society's responsibility for peace. John Eric Nordskog.

Southern Review. 3:673-92. Ap. '38. War machine examined. Lindsay Rogers.

*Spectator. 159:452-3. S. 17, '37. Armaments and peace. Guglielmo Ferrero.

Survey Graphic. 26:221-2. Ap. '37. Farce of the chandelier players. John Palmer Gavit.

Time. 31:9-10. F. 7, '38. Army and navy second to none.

Time. 31:18-19. F. 21, '38. Probe continued.

University of Texas Bulletin. No. 3638:11-220. O. 8, '36. Nationalization of munitions. Thomas A. Rousse.

Vital Speeches. 4:348-52. Mr. 15, '38. Pacifism, for and against. Alfred Salter; Wickham Steed.

*Washington Information Service of the National Peace Conference. 1:1-10. Je. 1, '38. Major trends in American foreign policy; Congressional digest.

Womans Press. 32:26-7+. Mr. '38. Law in the world order. Clyde Eagleton.

Yale Review. n.s. 27:790-800. Je. '38. If world war comes again. Leon Trotsky.

AFFIRMATIVE REFERENCES
BOOKS AND PAMPHLETS

Battleship. 24p. mimeo. U.S. War Dept. Wash. D.C. '38[?].

Hartley, Livingston. Is America afraid? 462p. Prentice-Hall Inc. N.Y. '37.

Potts, Adam E. A call to preparedness. *In* Quigley, Harold S. Peace or war? a conference. p. 162-78. (Day and Hour ser. Vol. 17 & 18) Univ. of Minnesota Press. Minneapolis. Je. '37.

Sisson, Mrs. Vinton Earl. National defense through patriotic education. 12p. mimeo. Institute of Public Affiairs, Univ. of Virginia. Charlottesville. Jl. 14, '37.

Statement of the chief of naval operations on the bill H.R. 9218. 15p. mimeo. Ja. 31, '38. U.S. War Dept. Wash. D.C. Ja. 31, '38.

PERIODICALS

Accountant (Lond) 97:719-22. N. 27, '37. Some notes on rearmament. J. H. Jones.

American Mercury. 42:173-80. O. '37. Disarmament hoax. Fletcher Pratt.

*Ancient Wisdom. 4:5. Mr. '38. War clouds over America. L. W. Rogers.

Atlantic Monthly. 161:495-503. Ap. '38. Peace and the navy. Dudley W. Knox.

China Weekly Review. 74:74. S. 21, '35. China serves as a horrible example for arms campaign in America.

Collier's. 98:74. N. 14, '36. Struggle for peace.

Collier's. 99:66. Ja. 16, '37. Sea race.

Collier's. 99:56+. F. 27, '37. Pacific fortress. Jim Marshall.

Collier's. 100:86. O. 16, '37. Face the danger.

Collier's. 101:66. F. 19, '38. Billions for defense.

*Congressional Record. 83: (current) 7299-7326. Ap. 19, '38. Naval expansion program. David I. Walsh.

Congressional Record. 83: (current) 7688-9. Ap. 26, '38. Naval authorization bill. Finly H. Gray.

Congressional Record. 83: (current) 8998-9. My. 12, '38. Place of Alaska in United States defense and economics. Anthony J. Dimond.

Congressional Record. 83: (current) 9182-3. My. 16, '38. America must increase its air forces.

Contemporary Review. 151:385-92. Ap. '37. Rearmament. Archibald Sinclair.

Current History. 46:43-5. Ag. '37. Arms over Europe. Curt L. Heymann.

*Dynamic America. 6:10-14. Je. '38. Isolation or collective security. Walter Shaw.

Economist (Lond.) 131:467-8. My. 38, '38. Crisis averted.

Foreign Affairs. 16:388-400. Ap. '38. Alternative American policies in the Far East. Tyler Dennett.

Forum. 95:206-10. Ap. '36. Billions for defense. Gerald P. Nye.

Great Britain and the East. 50:177. F. 17, '38. What war in the Pacific would mean. R. T. Barrett.

Literary Digest. 125:16-17. F. 12, '38. Warning to peace-at-any-price groups. Richard E. Byrd.

Nation. 144:200. F. 20, '37. Neutrality makes wars.

Nation. 145:643-5. D. 11, '37. Left prepares for war.
Ludwig Lore.

New Republic. 95:32, 39-42. My. 18, '38. Call to arms;
with editorial comment. Lewis Mumford.

New York Times. p. 1, 4. Ja. 29, '38. National defense
message to Congress. Franklin D. Roosevelt.

New York Times. Sec. 4. p. 5. F. 20, '38. Our big navy
plan is liked; South Americans see it as a protection
for themselves against a possible aggressor. John W.
White.

New York Times. p. 12. Mr. 8, '38. Speech before
House of Commons. Neville Chamberlain.

Scientific American. 158:137, 166. Mr. '38. Better naval
defense.

Spectator (Lond.) 157:143-4. Jl. 24, '36. Preparation
for war. H. Kethbridge Alexander.

Vital Speeches. 2:179-82. D. 16, '35. What is an adequate navy? H. L. Roosevelt.

Vital Speeches. 3:181-4. Ja. 1, '37. Our national air
defense. O. Westover.

Vital Speeches. 4:357-9. Ap. 1, '38. Naval preparedness, what road shall we take? Reginald R. Belknap.

Vital Speeches. 4:372-5. Ap. 1, '38. True pacifism;
righteousness at any cost. C. H. Woodward.

Vital Speeches. 4:403-6. Ap. 15, '38. Whither America?
Louis Johnson.

Yale Review. n.s. 27:333-47. D. '37. Navies and national policy. Melvin T. Talbot.

Yale Review. n.s. 27:649-63. Je. '38. After Geneva: the
defense of the peace. Walter Lippmann.

Negative References
Books and Pamphlets

Atkinson, Henry A. Prelude to peace. 222p. Harper
& Bros. N.Y. '37.

Blumenfield, Frank B. Blueprint for fascism. 23p. American League Against War and Fascism. 268 4th Av. N.Y. F. '37.

Boeckel, Florence. What is our national defense policy. 16p. National Council for Prevention of War. 532 17th St. N.W. Wash. D.C. Ja. 1, '37.

Buell, Raymond Leslie & Goslin, Ryllis Alexander. War drums and peace plans. 38p. Foreign Policy Assn. 8 W. 40th St. N.Y. '36.

Butler, Nicholas Murray. The Family of nations; its needs and its problems. 400p. Charles Scribner's Sons. N.Y. '38.

Eddy, Sherwood & Page, Kirby. What shall we do about war? 96p. (World Problem Ser. no. 20) Eddy & Page. 347 Madison Ave. N.Y. n.d.

Engelbrecht, H. C. Revolt against war. 367p. Dodd, Mead & Co. N.Y. '37.

*Fenwick, Charles G. Moral and legal bases of international peace. 6p. mimeo. Institute of Public Affairs, Univ. of Va. Charlottesville. Jl. 9, '37.

Griffin, Jonathan. Alternative to rearmament. 215p. Macmillan & Co. Lond. '36.

Hallgren, Mauritz A. Tragic fallacy; a study of America's war policies. 474p. Alfred A. Knopf. N.Y. '37.

Huxley, Aldous. Encyclopaedia of pacifism. 104p. Harper & Bros. N.Y. '37.

Institute of International Affairs. Proceedings. 12:194-201. '34. Moral disarmament and the traffic in arms. J. Eugene Harley.

Jacks, L. P. Co-operation or coercion. 153p. E. P. Dutton & Co. N.Y. '38.

Manifesto against war: armistice day message. Church Peace Union. 70 Fifth Av. N.Y. N. '34.

Nationalization of munitions. 10p. mim. National Council for Prevention of War. 532 17th St. N.W., Wash. D.C. Ap. 17, '37.

Noble, Elizabeth. Billions for bullets. 23p. American League Against War and Fascism. 268 4th Av. N.Y. F. '37.

Nobody can attack us. 2p. National Council for Prevention of War. Wash. D.C. '38.

Noel-Baker, Philip. Private manufacture of armaments. 574p. Oxford Univ. Press. N.Y. '37.

O'Brien, John A. Church and disarmament. 31p. Our Sunday visitor. Huntington, Ind. n.d.

Page, Kirby. Must we go to war? 278p. Farrar & Rinehart. N.Y. '37.

Raushenbush, Stephen and Raushenbush, Joan. War madness. 190p. National Home Library Foundation. Wash. D.C. '37.

Russell, Bertrand. Which way to peace. 224p. Michael Joseph. Lond. '36.

Watkins, Arthur Charles. America stands for pacific means. 142p. National Capital Press. Wash. D.C. '37.

Important books, pamphlets, and materials for teachers and for school libraries. p. 122-3.

PERIODICALS

Adult Education. 10:150-6. D. '37. National will to peace. Norman Angell.

American Mercury. 38:299-310. Jl. '36. Highly moral causes of war. Lawrence Dennis.

American Mercury. 44:211-16. Je. '38. Down the rathole; epidemic of armament for defense. Albert Jay Nock.

American Scholar. 6, no. 3:334-44. Summer '37. Fight the good fight? A. J. Muste.

Asia. 38:230-2. Ap. '38. America plays a risky game. John T. Flynn.

Atlantic Monthly. 157:138-49. F. '36. We militarize. Oswald Garrison Villard.

Christian Century. 55:132. F. 2, '38. Seventy million dollar battleships.

Christian Century. 55:195. F. 16, '38. Admiral Leahy testifies.

Christian Century. 55:271-2. Mr. 2, '38. Is youth to be betrayed again? Jean Beaven Abernethy.

Christian Century. 55:294-6. Mr. 9, '38. Can naval building bring prosperity?

Christian Century. 55:397-9. Mr. 30, '38. We did it once. Hubert Herring.

Christian Century. 55:404. Mr. 30, '38. How curb the President? Irvine M. Dungan.

Christian Century. 55:550-1. My. 4, '38. Super-navy is not for defense!

*Christian Science Monitor Weekly Magazine Section. p. 1-2. Mr. 10, '37. Preparedness for peace. Gerald P. Nye.

Congressional Record. 83: (current) 2549-50. F. 14, '38. Navy for defense, but not for aggression. Hamilton Fish.

*Congressional Record. 83: (current) 7230. Ap. 18, '38. War or peace. Knute Hill.

Congressional Record. 83: (current) 1938. Je. 2, '38. Why additional battleships? William Lemke.

Congressional Record. 83: (current) 12687-8. Je. 16, '38. How to keep America out of war. Hamilton Fish.

Congressional Record. 83: (current) 12963-74. Je. 22, '38. Keep the American flag flying in the western hemisphere. Ernest Lundeen.

Current History. 46:32-6. Ag. '37. How dangerous is Japan? Marc T. Greene.

Current History. 48:45-9. Ja. '38. Arming the good neighbors. Genaro Arbaiza.

Dynamic America. 5:15-17. Ja. '38. World peace insurance. Edward G. Bernard.

Dynamic America. 6:10-12. Jl. '38. Implications of collective security. James Lee Randolph.

Hibbert Journal. 34:493-509. Jl. '36. Demilitarized League of Nations. L. P. Jacks.

Homiletic Review. 107:347-50. My. '34. What now, preacher? Lucia Ames Mead.

International Conciliation. 338:114-18. Mr. '38. Program recommended by the thirteenth Conference on the Cause and Cure of War.

International Conciliation. 339:156-73. Ap. '38. Is world peace an attainable ideal? George M. Stratton.

Labour (Lond.) 4:61. N. '36. Democratic national defense or professional militarism? Thomas Kennedy.

Labour (Lond.) 4:72-3. N. '36. Plotters against world peace. R. H. Tawney.

Labour (Lond.) 4:138-9. F. '37. Don't despair of disarmament; the League can still lead the way to peace. Morgan Jones.

Labour Monthly. 19:411-15. Jl. '37. Rearmament and overproduction. John Knight.

Labour Monthly. 19:564-9. S. '37. Rearmament and labour conditions. John Knight.

Labour Monthly. 19:634-8. O. '37. International consequences of rearmament. John Knight.

Nation. 142:436-7. Ap. 8, '36. America is arming.

Nation. 144:240. F. 27, '37. Issues and men. Oswald Garrison Villard.

Nation. 144:524-5. My. 8, '37. Are we safe from war?

Nation. 144:677. Je. 12; 145:349. O. 2, '37; 146:45. Ja. 8; 100. Ja. 22; 157. F. 5; 184. F. 12; 209. F. 19, '38. Issues and men. Oswald Garrison Villard.

Nation. 146:200-3. F. 19, '38. Big-navy stuff; War is in the air. Sherwood Anderson.

National Education Association. Journal. 26:281-2. D. '37. Shall we go on making little soldiers?

New Republic. 90:97-8. Mr. 3, '37. Britain's navy— and ours.

New Republic. 93:328-30. Ja. 26, '38. Memorandum on national policy. Bruce Bliven.

New York Herald Tribune. p. 17. Jl. 12, '38. Mobilization of Europe. Walter Lippmann.

Newsweek. 11:40. Mr. 28, '38. Drifting toward war. Raymond Moley.

Nineteenth Century. 122:140-51. Ag. '37. How to make our armaments useless. Norman Angell.

Review of Reviews. 91:44-6. F. '35. War and the munitions racket. Linley Gordon.

Review of Reviews. 95:54-5. My. '37. Pacifism means peace. Harry Emerson Fosdick.

Rotarian. 50:8-10. My. '37. Way to peace. George Paish.

Scholastic. 32:2. F. 26, '38. Let's not kid ourselves.

*Social Science. 11:332-4. O. '36. Patriotism, Inc. James Edwin Edwards.

South Atlantic Quarterly. 36:121-36. Ap. '37. Pacific policy for the Pacific. David Y. Thomas.

Spectator. 156:981. My. 29, '36. Pacifism and rearmament. Leyton Richards.

Survey Graphic. 27:222-3+. Ap. '38. Long shadow of John Paul Jones. Victor Weybright.

Vital Speeches. 4:376-7. Ap. 1, '38. Millions for what? cost of war preparation. Merlin Hull.

War—What For.
A new anti-war magazine published by The Keep America Out of War Committee, 112 E. 19th St. N.Y. '38.

World Alliance for International Friendship Through the Churches and Church Peace Union. News Letter.
Previously Church Peace Union and World Alliance for International Friendship Through the Churches. News Letter. See recent numbers, specially 1937, 1938.

Woman's Home Companion. 65:22+. Ap. '38. America's defenses. Mauritz A. Hallgren.

GENERAL DISCUSSION

QUARANTINING WAR [1]

The present reign of terror and international lawlessness began a few years ago. It began thru unjustified interference in the international affairs of other nations or the invasion of alien territory in violation of treaties, and has now reached a stage where the very foundations of civilization are seriously threatened.

The landmarks and traditions which have marked the progress of civilization toward a condition of law, order and justice are being wiped away.

Without a declaration of war and without warning or justification of any kind, civilians, including women and children, are being ruthlessly murdered with bombs from the air.

In times of so-called peace ships are being attacked and sunk by submarines without cause or notice. Nations are fomenting and taking sides in civil warfare in nations that have never done them any harm. Nations claiming freedom for themselves deny it to others.

Innocent peoples and nations are being cruelly sacrificed to a greed for power and supremacy which is devoid of all sense of justice and humane consideration.

To paraphrase a recent author: "Perhaps we foresee a time when men, exultant in the technique of homicide, will rage so hotly over the world that every precious thing will be in danger, every book and picture and harmony, every treasure garnered thru two

[1] From address of President Franklin D. Roosevelt, at Chicago, October 5, 1937. *New York Times.* p. 16. October 6, 1937.

millenniums, the small, the delicate, the defenseless—all will be lost or wrecked or utterly destroyed."

If those things come to pass in other parts of the world, let no one imagine that America will escape, that it may expect mercy, that this Western Hemisphere will not be attacked and that it will continue tranquilly and peacefully to carry on the ethics and the arts of civilization.

The peace-loving nations must make a concerted effort in opposition to those violations of treaties and those ignorings of humane instinct which today are creating a state of international anarchy and instability from which there is no escape through mere isolation or neutrality.

Those who cherish their freedom and recognize and respect the equal right of their neighbors to be free and live in peace must work together for the triumph of law and moral principles in order that peace, justice and confidence may prevail in the world.

There must be a return to a belief in the pledged word, in the value of a signed treaty. There must be recognition of the fact that national morality is as vital as private morality.

There is a solidarity and interdependence about the modern world, both technically and morally, which makes it impossible for any nation completely to isolate itself from economic and political upheavals in the rest of the world, especially when such upheavals appear to be spreading and not declining.

There can be no stability or peace either within nations or between nations except under laws and moral standards adhered to by all. International anarchy destroys every foundation for peace. It jeopardizes either the immediate or the future security of every nation, large or small.

It is, therefore, a matter of vital interest and concern to the people of the United States that the sanctity of international treaties and the maintenance of international morality be restored.

The overwhelming majority of the peoples and nations of the world today want to live in peace.

They seek the removal of barriers against trade.

They want to exert themselves in industry, in agriculture and in business, that they may increase their wealth thru the production of wealth-producing goods rather than striving to produce military planes and bombs and machine guns and cannon for the destruction of human lives and useful property.

In those nations of the world which seem to be piling armament on armament for purposes of aggression, and those other nations which fear acts of aggression against them and their security, a very high proportion of the national income is being spent directly for armaments. It runs from 30 to as high as 50 per cent. The peace, the freedom and the security of 90 per cent of the population of the world is being jeopardized by the remaining 10 per cent who are threatening a breakdown of all international order and law.

Surely the 90 per cent who want to live in peace under law and in accordance with moral standards that have received almost universal acceptance thru the centuries, can and must find some way to make their will prevail.

The situation is definitely of universal concern. The questions involved relate not merely to violation of specific provisions of particular treaties; they are questions of war and of peace, of international law, and especially of principles of humanity. It is true that they involve definite violations of agreements, and especially of the Covenant of the League of Nations, the Briand-Kellogg Pact and the Nine-Power Treaty. But they also involve problems of world economy, world security and world humanity.

It is true that the moral consciousness of the world must recognize the importance of removing injustices and well-founded grievances; but at the same time it must be aroused to the cardinal necessity of honoring sanctity of treaties, of respecting the rights and liberties of others and of putting an end to acts of international aggression.

It seems to be unfortunately true that the epidemic of world lawlessness is spreading.

When an epidemic of physical disease starts to spread, the community approves and joins in a quarantine of the patients in order to protect the health of the community against the spread of the disease.

It is my determination to pursue a policy of peace and to adopt every practicable measure to avoid involvement in war.

It ought to be inconceivable that in this modern era, and in the face of experience, any nation could be so foolish and ruthless as to run the risk of plunging the whole world into war by invading and violating, in contravention of solemn treaties, the territory of other nations that have done them no real harm and which are too weak to protect themselves adequately. Yet the peace of the world and the welfare and security of every nation is today being threatened by that very thing.

War is a contagion, whether it be declared or undeclared. It can engulf the original scene of hostilities. We are determined to keep out of war, yet we cannot insure ourselves against the disastrous effects of war and the dangers of involvement. We are adopting such measures as will minimize our risk of involvement, but we cannot have complete protection in a world of disorder in which confidence and security have broken down.

If civilization is to survive, the principles of the Prince of Peace must be restored. Shattered trust between nations must be revived.

Most important of all, the will for peace on the part of peace-loving nations must express itself to the end that nations that may be tempted to violate their agreements and the rights of others will desist from such a cause. There must be positive endeavors to preserve peace.

SPIRIT OF INTERNATIONAL LAW [2]

Two decades ago the concepts of peace based upon competitive armaments seemed to have been buried under the wreckage caused by an otherwise utterly destructive world conflict. Out of that purgatory there emerged a profound realization that a new basis must be found for relations among nations. There arose a faith and a hope that a new spirit and a new system would come to prevail in the international structure of the world. The negotiation of numerous multilateral treaties and agreements and the creation of appropriate regional and even world-wide organizations were important steps in the direction of a system of true international cooperation— of a world order based upon international law; upon the principles of equality, justice, fairness, and mutual respect among nations; upon progressive disarmament; upon a determination to substitute for war as an arbiter of international relations observance of the pledged word and willingness to compose international differences by pacific means.

The fact that today these efforts to establish thru international cooperation a world order under law are being challenged again by the doctrine of armed force and lawless self-aggrandizement leads many people to the belief that the idea and principles of a peaceful and orderly world have proved to be unworkable. This belief is the product of a dangerous and unfortunate weakening of confidence. The challenge itself has arisen, because the recent years have been characterized by a

[2] From address of Secretary of State Cordell Hull at Nashville, Tenn., June 3, 1938. *Congressional Record.* 83:10764. June 3, 1938.

disastrous lowering of standards of conduct on the part of both individuals and nations— by a relapse in the spiritual and moral strength and driving power of vast masses of mankind and a consequent faltering of the march of human progress. Such relapses and such falterings have occurred before. That they are temporary in nature is amply attested by the lesson of history.

In the circumstances of today, it is a part of wisdom and prudence for a great nation like ours to provide adequately for its national defense. Security is essential, and peace is better than war, even when under conditions of grave emergency, it has to be temporarily assured by adequate national armaments. But peace thus maintained is precarious and unenduring—a makeshift, at best. Stable and durable peace can be achieved only thru the universal enthronement of the spirit of respect for law and thru a resumption of determined efforts toward international cooperation—both of which in our lifetime have revealed themselves as attainable realities. Not until it is proved that these are no longer effective world forces, will there be any justifiable grounds for the belief that armed force, and armed force alone, will rule international relations, and that, therefore, the outlook for peace, progress, and civilization is devoid of all hope.

At this crucial juncture of history, it is our nation's duty to itself to make its appropriate contribution toward preservation and advancement of the principles of international law and of the orderly and cooperative processes of international relations, which have evolved with, and have in turn promoted, the development of civilization. Toward that end we should maintain and strengthen our own adherance to the principles and processes of international law. We should exert all moral force of which we are capable toward influencing other nations to work for the same end and to accept and employ the civilized practices of pacific settlement in connection with

such controversies as may arise among them. We should
be prepared to aid, and, in every practicable way, resort
to such peaceful means of settlement. Within the limitations of our traditional policies, and without entangling
alliances or involvements, we should cooperate, sincerely
and resolutely, with like-minded nations working toward
the same goal for which we ourselves are striving.

There are important and concrete steps which can
and should be taken without delay to reverse the present
disastrous trends in international relations.

With the world still in the throes of a profound
economic dislocation, we are prepared to join with other
nations in directing every effort toward the restoration
and strengthening of sound and constructive international
economic relationships.

With the world groaning under the burden of mounting armaments, we are prepared to join with other
nations in moving resolutely toward bringing about an
effective agreement on limitation and progressive reduction of armaments.

With the use of armed force assuming the aspect of
scarcely imaginable brutality, we are prepared to join
with other nations in resuming and vigorously carrying
forword the work, so auspiciously begun at The Hague
two generations ago, of humanizing by common agreement the rules and practices of warfare.

We are prepared to join with other nations in ex-
ploring all other methods of revitalizing the spirit of
international cooperation and in making use of every
practicable means of giving it substance and reality thru
the numberless forms of concrete application of such
principles of international, political, economic, and
cultural relations as those to which I have referred.

All these are necessary and constructive steps in
which a free and powerful nation like ours can and
should participate wholeheartedly, if durable peace is
to be firmly established and civilization is to survive and

advance. There is desperate need in our country, and in every country, of a strong and united public opinion in support of such a renewal and demonstration of faith in the possibility of a world order based on law and international cooperative effort. When such public opinion has developed and when the momentous issue of today—the fateful decision as to whether relations among nations shall be governed by armed force or by cooperation and order under law—is clearly understood and visualized, there will be no insuperable difficulty in finding acceptable ways and means of achieving the desired end.

KEEPING OUT OF WAR [3]

The ways and means of keeping out of war can be classified in four general groups and eleven different categories, ranging all the way from the stout-hearted big-navy people to the meek but equally resolute non-resisters.

The first group is aggressive and rather military in tenor. There are four categories of method here: national defense, Anglo-American alliance, Pan-American alliance, and defense of democracy. The old-fashioned big-navy patriots are still with us, believing that we must speak to nations who scoff at peace in their own hard language. Again, those who advocate a naval alliance with the English-speaking commonwealths, to police the world, make a very strong case indeed. A Pan-American military combination, however, seems somewhat too idealistic. The fourth class, those who believe we must keep out of war only until democracy is threatened, concede that our historic emotions, when democracy is menaced on another continent, will

[3] From article by Harry Goddard Leach, Editor. *Forum.* 98:49-50. August, 1937. The *Forum* had previously invited various leaders of public opinion to express themselves on the proper means of keeping America out of the next great war. This editorial is largely a resumé of the replies.

overwhelm any mechanical devices we set up to restrain
ourselves. For this school of thought it is the function
of the United States to defend democracy wherever it
needs defense, whether at home or abroad.

The second group of war preventionists subscribes
to the new neutrality doctrine. It includes three categories: locking the gate, mandatory embargoes, and
discretionary neutrality. This group is most vocative at
present and has produced the recent so-called neutrality
laws in Congress. The extreme isolationists would have
no intercourse with warring nations. Under the Pact of
Paris we have a right to treat any belligerent nation as
an outlaw. Such a formula is simple but one likely to
lead to economic chaos. The Secretary of Agriculture
estimates that, if we could not sell to a world at war, the
government would have to spend astronomical sums keeping us employed domestically. Similarly, mandatory
embargoes against warring nations, just as they seem,
would lead to all sorts of ill will and economic disloca-
tions. They would be hard on Mr. Hull's treaties. We
can imagine a battle between two belligerent fleets in
one of our own harbors struggling to get possession of
an American barrel of flour. It remains to be seen
whether the new neutrality will keep us out of war any
longer than the old formula of freedom of the seas.

If we are to outlaw trade with nations that commit
the folly of war, the aggressor nation deserves severer
treatment than the nation attacked. It would be better
to make embargoes discretionary and leave it to the
executive to use his best judgment in the national interest. For every new war is pretty sure to offer situations
so novel and extraordinary that no law can anticipate
them.

The third group of American war preventionists
advocates economic rather than military pressure. There
are two categories, those who recommend sanctions
under the Pact of Paris and those who would have us

strengthen the League of Nations by joining it and employing sanctions against aggressor countries. The first set of students calls to mind that sanctions might have been employed effectively to keep Japan out of Manchuria, if Sir John Simon had been willing to cooperate with Secretary Stimson. The League of Nations adherents point to the first experiment in sanctions, employed against Italy, and believe it would have been more successful had the United States participated at the first invasion of Ethiopian territory.

The fourth war-prevention group consists of idealists: those who believe that the only hope of peace is a new social order based on some form of socialism or cooperation and the nonresisters, those who put conscience above country. They are in perpetual personal strike against war and prefer to suffer ignominies or death rather than engage in the traffic of mass slaughter.

Under what conditions have nations in our day avoided war? The Scandinavian countries succeeded in keeping out of the World war and yet kept their honor intact. What was their formula? Superior intelligence is, naturally, one complete answer. We observe also that these countries are relatively poor in natural resources and do not excite unduly the military greed of other powers. We notice further that the Scandinavians always succeed in being actively engaged in trade and that they traded vigorously during the World war with the belligerents as well as the neutrals, as long as they were permitted to do so. We realize again that they were actuated by a passion to keep out of war, an eagerness like that which now stirs the farms of our Middle West. The shipping of Norway suffered far more from German submarines than did our own, but the Norwegians were willing to endure the pangs of an outrageous fortune. In the last years of the war, when Sweden was forced on rations by the Allies and every neutral Swede had to tighten his belt, a Swedish envoy who came to America to beg for food for his countrymen declared that there had been every inducement to drag his country into the war but that his people had been free from war for one hundred years and were determined not to allow their fair fields again to be foolishly drenched by human blood.

The Danes, in the years before the World war, lived in dread that Germany would erupt across their borders instead of invading Belgium. A novel appeared, anonymously, giving the details of the German occupation of Denmark overnight. The chief political issue at that time was national defense. There were four leading parties, four points of view. The conservatives wished to make every sacrifice for greater fortifications. The liberals wanted merely to maintain the existing military organization strong enought to keep off a German invasion until the English could arrive to save Denmark. The radicals were for demolishing existing forts because it was futile for Denmark to hold out in a military way. Patriotism should be manifested thru superior civilization. "Our culture," they said, "will preserve us." The fourth party, the socialists, likewise voted against national defense. Their argument, however, was that there was to be no war because their friends, the socialists of Germany, would refuse to take up arms.

It was a compromise that won out in Denmark before the World war, much as it is the new neutrality compromise under which we are operating today in the United States. The direction is toward pacifism, but the military arm is being kept intact. In the World war, Denmark was spared largely thru the intelligent trading spirit of her people, who sold their butter to England and their cows to Germany until the last gasp, when they were compelled by the belligerents to slaughter their swine. The Danes endured many insults. Their diplomacy had to be as keen as the balance of an acrobat on a flying trapeze. But they emerged with peace and

honor. And no landscape is more dotted with flags of
patriotism than that of peace-loving Denmark.

A combination of superior education, reasonableness,
and the economic open door is responsible for the success of the Scandinavians in practicing the arts of peace
in a war-ridden world.

There are several international moods and programs
that we are practicing today which in the end may contribute more to the cause of peace than any mechanical
apparatus that we set up. First of these is the conference. Americans take kindly to conference, for we are
a nation of committees. If we can keep prospective
belligerents in conference long enough, their wrath will
eventually cool, and they will find grounds of agreement.
The Washington naval holiday was a magnificent achievement, altho it proved to be only an interlude. Every
hour spent in conference that puts off war another hour
is not in vain. Conference eventually wears down
irreconcilable points of view.

We were a signatory to the Pact of Paris. It has
not prevented war but it remains forever another moral
obstruction against war.

In recent years the conferences to limit armaments in
which we have participated have been discouraging to
idealists. Yet even in the last conference some result
remained, after the withdrawal of other nations, when
Great Britain and the United States agreed to exchange
their naval blueprints before proceeding to new construction. With unperturbed and smiling patience our
ambassador-at-large, Mr. Norman Davis, goes from conference to conference, urging limitation and maintaining
the constructive attitude that, however imminent it seems,
there is actually to be no war.

International conferences should never adjourn but
should labor day and night for the community of nations.
At the present moment there should be sitting intermin-
ably an international economic conference bent on open-

ing access to raw commodities, improving trade, and stabilizing currencies. The world needs a "world dollar."

A second auxiliary force for peace is the cultivation of good will. President Roosevelt has capitalized that salutary emotion in his "good neighbor" policy. It does seem inexplicable that, after two thousand years of Christianity, two Christian nations can fight each other. They could not, of course, do so if their religion were more than skin deep.

The third auxiliary technique of the peace movement is education. In general, greater enlightenment means less war. Temporarily, of course, it is not so; for we let the elaborate results of research, such as explosives, gases, bacteria, get into the hands of the wrong people. In the long run peace is but a by-product of education, which will go on forever, cycles after war has been banished from our little planet.

The fourth auxiliary to the peace movement is, of course, international trade. In the kindly Victorian days, when British trade was at its zenith and the missionary spirit of good will abroad in all lands, the world had no time to bother about big wars. Today armaments are at a new maximum; today trade is more relentlessly restricted than ever before in the world's history.

Peace is a majority concept of the human race. What focus and direction is discernible in this confusion of counsel? Is it armament so effective that war becomes unthinkable? Or is it nonresistance and strikes against arms on the part of a majority of individuals? No, a drift to either of these extremes is unlikely.

Miracles have happened. It is somewhat of a miracle that any animals as turbulent, pugnacious, selfish, controversial, stupid, unreasonable as human beings have ever been able to organize themselves into states where human happiness is given a chance to increase. But what are the mechanical devices that ensure this gradual integration of good will and intelligence? They are,

are they not, the courts and the police? In domestic relations we are not yet ready for a Utopian system of courtless and policeless society. In international relations we have not yet even reached the stage of a universal court and police system. But it is in that practical direction that efforts for world peace are tending.

No gesture toward peace is futile, not even parades by peace-loving women in the center of the corn belt, far removed from international frontiers. Our recent neutrality legislation is not futile. No arms conference is futile, even tho it may not succeed in limiting armaments by as much as a single gun. And the process of daily education in reasonableness and intelligent good will must be encouraged in every school in every land under whatever form of government.

NAVY AS AN INSTRUMENT OF DIPLOMACY [4]

A few years ago Mr. Charles Francis Adams, then Secretary of the Navy, made the somewhat ponderous observation that the navy "is the silent assistant which aids diplomacy . . . and which exerts pressure in furtherance of national policy." In the tranquil atmosphere of 1930 this obvious truth was allowed to pass without comment. Outwardly the world was at peace. The Five Power Naval conference then in session in London was engrossed with mathematical formulae which were often confused with peace and disarmament. The admirals were too deeply involved in their controversy over the relative merits of six-inch and eight-inch gun cruisers to trouble themselves with political imponderables. The diplomats were too occupied with arbitrary ratios to note the dark clouds on the distant horizon. And Ameri-

[4] From article by William T. Stone, Vice-President, Foreign Policy Association. *Amerasia.* 2:63-7. March, 1938.

can public opinion, distracted by the simultaneous advent of midget golf and the stock market crash, was in no mood to be bothered by anything so utterly remote as the navy and national policy.

By the winter of 1938, events in the Far East had thrust the navy into the forefront of a bitter debate on foreign policy. War in China had jeopardized American lives and property. American ships and mission compounds had been bombed. An American gunboat had been bombed. An American gunboat had been sunk. An American diplomat had been slapped. Stern notes had been dispatched from Washington to Tokyo. Three American cruisers had steamed to Singapore to participate in the ceremonies at the opening of Britain's mighty naval base. An $800,000,000 naval expasion program had been rushed to Congress. And American public opinion, distracted by fears of foreign wars and domestic depression, had become suddenly aware of navies and national policy.

But the relation between navies and national policy was scarcely more clear in 1938 than it had been in 1930. Questions had been asked and answers given. But too many questions and answers had missed the mark. Senator Borah, his suspicions aroused by outward evidence of British "intrigue," had bluntly demanded, "What is American foreign policy?"—a question not easily answered at any time. Hiram Johnson, aroused to action by the implications of "secret consultations" in London, introduced his resolution asking the Secretary of State "to advise the Senate whether or not any alliance, agreement or understanding exists or is contemplated with Great Britain relating to war or the possibility of war"—a simple wording to which Mr. Hull was able to reply with an immediate and emphatic "no."

If the Senate skirmish was unsatisfactory the public hearings conducted by the House Naval Affairs Committee on Mr. Roosevelt's expansion program were equally unproductive. Admiral Leahy, on the witness stand for more than a week, successfully parried all questions relating to foreign policy with a series of sharp negatives: the expansion program was solely for "defense against attack on our shores" and "outlying possessions"; it was long overdue and was called for by the rearmament programs of other powers. There was nothing in the program that would permit of "aggressive action" or a policy of "policing the world" or "projecting an attack against the territory of any other naval power." It was not a move in the direction of "Anglo-American domination of the seas."

To these disarming negatives Admiral Leahy added other more positive assertions: (a) It would require "at least three times the proposed increase" to prepare for aggressive action in the Far East. (b) The maintenance of the United States fleet in the Pacific was in line with the "long-standing policy" of the Navy "to maintain a single fleet in one ocean." (c) The proposed increase is not sufficient "to guard against attack on both shores at once."

Despite the apparent contradictions in the public record, however, a few factors seem to be reasonably clear. It is obvious that the navy is today, as it has been in the past, an instrument of national policy; that the navy is being used to support diplomacy; that the Roosevelt armament program is a product of political conditions in both Europe and Asia at this moment; that the potential enemies are certainly not Switzerland, Sweden or Siam, but are possibly Japan, Germany and Italy; that the ability of the navy to perform certain strategic missions will not be altered by the expansion program for at least three or four years when the new ships are placed in commission about 1941-42; and that even then the relative situation may not be profoundly altered.

Other factors in the equation are less easy to catalog. As one observer puts it, the problem is one in which "every quantity is a variable, in which the ends are impossible of close estimate, the means are insusceptible of pragmatic calculation and even the debate is necessarily shrouded in diplomatic reticence." Perhaps, however, the problem can be simplified by classifying the known and unknown quantities and by distinguishing between two separate functions of the navy as an instrument of policy; (a) the influence of the navy as an aid to diplomacy in "peaceful pressure" short of war and (b) the rôle of the navy if diplomacy fails to obtain its ends by peaceful means. Under the first category the mere existence of armed force may be employed to further specific diplomatic ends. Under the second function the navy must be in a position to carry out the measures assigned to it by force of arms.

If the diplomatic objectives are obscure, the strategic factors are relatively well known. From these known quantities it is reasonably clear that the United States cannot be attacked in the Western hemisphere by any single power and cannot single-handed carry successful offensive operations to the Far East. It is also reasonably clear that Great Britain cannot contemplate extensive naval operations alone in the Western Pacific, and probably cannot defend Hongkong against a direct Japanese attack. Finally, Japan, while unable to challenge America's dominant position in the Alaska-Hawaii-Panama triangle, remains itself dominant in the Western Pacific unless confronted with a hostile combination.

Nevertheless, there are plain indications that the strategic balance in the Pacific has been shifting perceptibly for some time, to the detriment of Japan. Under the Washington Conference agreements of 1922, Japan was given "the keys to the Western Pacific" in the form of naval supremacy in that area. When the balance was upset with the invasion of Manchuria in 1931, the Western powers were unable to enter an effective challenge, and for the next four years, or until 1935, Japanese dominance in the Western Pacific increased steadily. Since 1935, however, her position has been gradually weakened by shifts in the balance of power; the concentration of a powerful Soviet army of 350,000 men, with at least 1,000 airplanes, in eastern Siberia; the launching of Britain's huge rearmament program and the completion of the naval base at Singapore; and the building up of the American navy, first, to the "treaty strength" and now to even higher levels.

The relative balance in the Pacific, moreover, is intimately linked with the balance of power in Europe, where Britain is faced with the necessity of meeting any threat in the North Sea and the Mediterranean. If the present alignment persists, Britain will be compelled to maintain at least three capital ships as the core of a fairly strong fleet in the North Sea, and a powerful detachment to cooperate with the French navy in the Meditterranean. The present arrangement with France, which has demonstrated the clear superiority of the combined force over Italy, undoubtedly calls for from three to five British capital ships for Mediterranean duty. The British know that any major European crisis would compel them to mobilize an overwhelming force in the two danger zones nearest home, and would leave them almost defenseless in the Pacific. Nothing short of an Anglo-Italian settlement on the one hand, or rapprochement with Germany on the other, would permit the release of the necessary capital ships and auxiliaries for the projected Pacific fleet.

Many other qualifications might be added to the list, but these illustrations are sufficient to indicate the complexity of the problem. The "known factors" are offset by a host of "unknown," not the least of which are the diplomatic imponderables. Without attempting to fix the actual diplomatic objectives, however, it is at least possible to set down certain limits within which the navy is functioning as an instrument of diplomacy in the Far

East and to estimate the points beyond which it cannot function without grave risk.

To begin with it is perfectly clear that neither Great Britain nor the United States, acting alone, can defend its respective interests or influence a new Pacific settlement in Asia. The attempt would be disastrous, for it would project diplomatic objectives which cannot be carried out by the navy in a showdown. It is also apparent that an Anglo-American alliance or "understanding" is politically impossible at this time, and that "collective action" is meaningless today except in terms of joint action. Mr. Hull's answer to Senator Johnson was final, no doubt. But the very balance of forces in the Pacific encourages the States Department to pursue its "parallel action" with a view to making this balance an effective instrument of diplomacy. The steps taken since the *Panay* incident in mid-December suggest the method; first, consultations in London looking toward joint invocation of the "escalator" clause of the 1936 naval treaty and also exchange of information on distribution of forces in the Pacific. Second, the despatch of three American cruisers to Singapore for the ceremonies attending the completion of the naval base (incidentally, it is said that the date for the ceremonies was advanced by several months). Third, completion of plans for American naval maneuvers in the area of Samoa, 2,600 miles southwest of Hawaii, and the announcement by Admiral Leahy that the traditional defense line has been extended to include Samoa. Fourth, the timing of identic notes by the United States, Great Britain and France requesting information from Tokyo on naval building plans and extending an invitation to a new limitation conference.

There are two possible interpretations of these parallel steps. One is that the United States and Great Britain are preparing for a showdown with Japan in the near future, a view which was widely held in

Congressional circles in Washington during the first weeks of February. The secret London mission of Captain Ingersoll, Chief of the War Plans Division of the office of Naval operations, was taken to mean that plans were being laid for a long distance blockade of Japan to be enforced by joint action of the two fleets. The circumstantial evidence also included the new emphasis placed on Samoa by Admiral Leahy, and reports that plans for such a blockade had actually been prepared by the Navy Department in Washington and the British Admiralty in London. To make the plan effective, it was said, Great Britain would have to base at least six capital ships and the necessary auxiliaries at Singapore; the United States would be expected to employ its full complement of fifteen capital ships to patrol a line from the Aleutians, via Hawaii, to Samoa, where the American fleet would connect with a British line from Singapore.

The second interpretation is less sensational, but probably in closer accord with established facts. According to this thesis, American and British diplomacy is taking full advantage of the existing balance of forces to press toward a new Pacific settlement in which the Western powers will have a voice. It is using the two navies, plus the Soviet position in Eastern Siberia, plus Chinese resistance, to convince the Japanese moderates that a compromise settlement is inevitable in the end, and that the Western powers intend to have a voice in that settlement.

It is quite possible that neither of these interpretations is correct. The long distance blockade scheme has been officially denied. But the crucial question, in the absence of any clear statement of diplomatic objectives, is how far the navy can be used effectively, without involving the nation in war, and without risking defeat if diplomacy fails. The limits have already been indicated. The British and American fleets, acting in concert, are not in a position *today* to force a showdown with Japan; they may or may not be within the next six months, if the British Pacific fleet is based at Singapore. Hence any diplomatic move which forces a showdown before the balance has changed profoundly would be courting disaster. Embargoes, economic sanctions, long distance blockades or any other measures which invite reprisals are dangerous because they force a showdown which in the last analysis the navy and the nation are not prepared to meet. If the bluff is called, the diplomats would commit the American navy to a task beyond its capacity to perform. Hongkong is still vulnerable, despite the new fortifications. The Philippines are vulnerable. The American navy cannot operate in the Western Pacific, even with the aid of six British capital ships, without a strong naval base somewhere in the South Seas. And the British are still immobilized in Europe. Eventually, if diplomatic blunders led to war, the combination of forces would prevail against Japan, but at a cost which no man can estimate today.

On the other hand, a case can be made for the use of the navy as an instrument of wise diplomacy. The balance is shifting and in time a settlement may be in sight. But discretion remains the better part of valor, and wise diplomacy will not set up objectives which cannot be achieved by the means at its disposal. The question troubling the American people in February 1938 is whether they are being led by wise or blustering diplomacy.

FOR IMPREGNABLE DEFENSE [5]

The military policy of a state which harbors no aggressive designs, but seeks only its own security, should be based primarily on the geographical and political conditions (1) of the state itself; (2) of its immediate

[5] From article by Major George Fielding Eliot. *New Republic.* 94, pt. 2:240-9. March 30, 1938.

neighbors; (3) of other states which might conceivably wage war against it. Next it must take account of the military strength of other states, and of the resources at its own disposal. Finally it must be brought into consonance with the other branches of state policy—diplomatic, commercial and domestic.

Military policy must be flexible; for tho geographical conditions do not change, the other factors mentioned are subject to fluctuations. It must provide defense against aggression; but it must not go beyond this need, lest it arouse the fears of others and also impose a needless burden on the treasury. Above all, military policy should be directed on the basis of cold, calm realism. It is not a department of government that can afford to indulge in illusions.

It is in this spirit, then, that we propose to examine the basic features of sound military policy for the United States.

The principal geographic fact with which this policy begins is our isolation from other great military powers by two oceans. The only direct passage between these oceans is in our hands. In both oceans we have certain outposts which add greatly to our military strength; those in the Caribbean area cover the eastward approaches to the defile of Panama, those in the Pacific cover our western seaboard.

By land, to the north, lies Canada, a country with which we have maintained unbroken friendship for over a century. Her defense forces are extremely weak. To the south is Mexico, a country with which our relations have not always been good; but she has practically no navy, and her army is deficient in modern equipment.

This weakness of our neighbors may, however, be a source of peril to us, since they may be unable, if we are at war, to prevent a hostile power seizing in their territory a base for operations against us.

Below Mexico, the six republics of Central America lead us down to Panama; beyond is the great continent of South America. For more than a century, we have been committed to the defense of all this territory against foreign aggression; a policy now being transmuted into one of mutual defense, to which at least three of the countries in question can make substantial naval and military contributions. This policy is sound. It contributes to the security of the Western Hemisphere, serves to allay Latin American suspicions of our ultimate aims, and will increase our prestige and influence among our neighbors while diminishing that of European and Asiatic powers, to our unquestionable benefit. Here we have a striking example of the manner in which military, political and commercial policy go hand in hand.

Since any serious menace to our security must come across one or the other of the oceans, it follows that our navy is our first line of defense; our military policy must, therefore, be initially concerned with bases for the support of our fleet. In the truest sense, bases mean ships: no navy can function in war without bases for repair and supply, without secure harbors where it can find shelter behind guns and minefields, and from which it can issue forth to perform its various tasks. The essential features of a naval base are described by Admiral Mahan as strength, resources and position; a navy possessed of adequate bases can within a given theatre operate successfully with a smaller actual force in ships than one not so situated.

A naval base itself, however, and the forts which defend it, are only of use as a point of support for the fleet which operates from it. The fallacies that have grown up in this country around the term "coast defense" are based on a misconception of this principle. "Coast defense," in the true sense, is the business first of all of the navy, supported by its bases. The actual operations of the fleet in defending the coast may take place hundreds of miles away. The farther the enemy can be kept from our shores, the better has the navy performed its functions.

Our North Atlantic seaboard posseses two principal naval bases, those of Norfolk and New York; a fleet of adequate power operating from these bases can dominate the whole of the waters from Newfoundland to the Straits of Florida. Secondary naval bases on this coast are at Portsmouth, Boston, Philadelphia and Charleston; Narragansett Bay (which is strategically part of the New York base), New Bedford, Portland and Savannah posses harbor defenses.

As we reach the tip of Florida we approach the most important strategic area of our Atlantic Coast— the Caribbean Sea, with the great landlocked basin of the Gulf of Mexico behind it. The Caribbean is the antechamber to the Panama Canal; it is vital to us to possess naval dominance in this area. The principal entrances to the Caribbean from the Atlantic are the Windward Passage between Cuba and Haiti, thru which moves our enormous intercoastal traffic via Panama, and the Anegada Passage to the eastward of the Virgin Islands, carrying most of the European traffic for Panama. The Windward Passage—and indeed the whole Caribbean Sea—is dominated by our base at Guantanamo Bay, Cuba, where we are established by treaty; this central position has as outpost the position Puerto Rico-Culebra-St. Thomas, which watches the Anegada Passage and, lying a thousand miles to seaward, flanks any European approach to our eastern seaboard. Guantanamo is not a defended port; but it has an excellent and commodious harbor, and—by car-ferry from Tampa and the Cuba Railway—can be amply supplied from the continental United States. There are no seacoast fortifications at Puerto Rico or St. Thomas. Key West (whose fortifications are on an inactive status) watches the Straits of Florida; within the Gulf of Mexico is Pensacola, with fortifications and a great naval air base. Finally there are the formidable defenses of the Panama Canal itself, backed by mobile troops, aircraft and submarines.

Our position in the Caribbean, tho strong, is susceptable of improvement to the point of impregnability, if political considerations could permit us to acquire certain additional positions now belonging to the British Empire—say in exchange for a reduction in the war debt. This is a very complicated question and may present insuperable obstacles: it is mentioned here merely as a suggestion. First, Bermuda, lying well out in the Atlantic, is not now but may become in the near future within squadron bombing range (500 miles) of our Atlantic seaboard; it is defended, but might fall into the hands of an enemy. In our hands it would afford an excellent flanking position, in advance of St. Thomas, for operations against any enemy approaching our Atlantic Coast. The Bahamas, with their numerous landlocked lagoons, might afford a base for enemy seaplanes or submarines operating against our commerce in the Straits of Florida or the Windward Passage; in our hands they would cover both those channels and form a strong outer support to the Guantanamo position. From St. Thomas, the operating range of a fleet (2,500 miles, at the extreme—2,000 miles if the requirements of maneuvering must be considered) will hardly reach into the South Atlantic; if we held Barbados, such operations as we might have to undertake in support of our Pan-American mutual-defense commitments would be much facilitated. It would not be necessary to keep any of these islands but Bermuda in a permanent state of defense.

In any case, the fortifications of Key West should be increased and placed on an active status; Guantanamo also, as the key point to the whole area, should have

permanent defenses. As for the other outposts, they
could be quickly reached by Marine Corps base-defense
and anti-aircraft artillery from Quantico or Parris Island.
This is a much more economical and flexible system than
the permanent maintenance of considerable garrisons at
every point. A small increase in the Fleet Marine Force
—two battalions of base-defense and two of anti-aircraft
artillery—would be advisable.

The key position for our West Coast defense is
Hawaii. Here we maintain a large garrison, navy and
army air forces, strong seacoast defenses and the major
part of our submarines. The naval base here is capable
of repairing battleships. Two thousand miles to the
northward, the Aleutian chain runs out in a long finger
pointing toward Eastern Asia. Here a naval and air base
should be placed; it requires defenses against raiding
cruisers, and facilities for repairing and supplying planes
and small vessels. This position commands the "great
circle" route from Asia to America. Our little outpost
at Samoa is too far distant to be part of our defense
chain; the 4,500-mile interval between Panama and
Hawaii might better be covered by an outpost in the
Marquesas Islands, now French, if this could be ar-
ranged. The Galapagos Islands, belonging to Ecuador,
would also afford excellent facilities for covering the
Pacific approaches to Panama.

Behind this outer line, our Pacific coast has naval
bases at Puget Sound, Mare Island and San Diego; of
these only Puget Sound is a first-class naval arsenal with
facilities for repairing the largest ships. The eventual
construction of a major naval base on San Francisco Bay
should be considered. Portland and Los Angeles (San
Pedro) are defended ports.

The Philippine Islands form a salient in our defense
line—an enormous salient, stretching five thousand miles
across the ocean from our main advanced position at
Hawaii. These islands, in the opinion of most military

authorities, could not be defended against Japan; the difficulties of making war over such distances, commanded as they are by the Japanese mandated islands, would be all but insuperable. When Philippine independence becomes a fact, sound military judgment dictates the withdrawal of our garrison and naval shore establishment. Ships necessary for the protection of American lives and property in the Far East can be maintained there without a base, as for many decades before the battle of Manila Bay.

On the whole, then, it may be said that our maritime frontiers are readily defensible, indeed, all but unassailable: provided—and it is an all-important proviso—that to the positions are added a sufficient fleet to command the adjacent seas, extending to the southward to include the Panama Canal.

This brings up the question of possible antagonists. It takes from three to four years to build a battleship, two to three years to build a cruiser, at least eighteen months to build a destroyer. Hence a watchful eye on what other people are doing should afford us adequate knowledge of what naval force might be brought against us. We may assume that we are not likely to be at war with the British Empire or France. The Soviet Union has no high-seas navy. There remain, as possible foes, but three major naval powers: Japan, Italy and Germany. All of these nations have within recent years committed acts of brutal aggression against other states. The world is still echoing with the thud of Nazi boot-heels on the pavements of Vienna. Hence it is by no means unreasonable or unjust to regard these three countries with suspicion. Furthermore, these three nations have an agreement among themselves, passing under the name of an anti-Communist pact, but which there is some reason to suppose constitutes in fact a military alliance. Finally, with Japan, at least, our relations are decidedly strained because of events in the Far East.

We may, therefore, consider that our immediate Pacific defense problem is that of security against Japanese aggression being extended to our own vital defense area, defined by the basic points Dutch Harbor-Hawaii-Panama. The core of such aggression would be the Japanese battle fleet, which has a present strength of ten battleships, six aircraft-carriers, twelve eight-inch-gun cruisers, twenty-three light cruisers and a formidable flotilla of destroyers and submarines (including many of the latter type which can cross the Pacific and return without refueling).

About the new Japanese naval program there is considerable mystery; details have been carefully shielded. It probably includes three or four battleships of 43,000 tons (10,000 tons heavier than anything at present in our navy) plus a number of vessels of other types.

Our problem comes down to this: how large a fleet should we need, based on Hawaii, to prevent the incursion of this Japanese fleet into waters in which dominance is essential to our security?

The answer must be based on battleship strength, since, in oceanic operations especially, the battleship is the very foundation of naval power. The best proof of this is that all the major navies are building them—and many are nations which have no money to waste on expensive luxuries.

Weighing carefully all factors, it seems certain that a 20 per cent superiority over the Japanese in battle strength should afford a very comfortable margin for the defense of our Pacific waters. Just now the twelve battleships of our main fleet are sufficient; the completion of three more ships by Japan would require us to add four. This is based on the theory that the aggressor will strike with concentrated force at his selected moment, which may be when certain of our ships are in dockyard hands, or otherwise not immediately available. If we could make sure that this would not be so, the distance factor would make an even number of battleships sufficient.

We should, then, base our battleship program on a strength of sixteen ships for the Pacific. Our cruiser-and-destroyer program should look to the orderly replacement of obsolete craft now on the navy list. Our submarine force ought to be very considerably increased, not only in long-range fleet submarines but to provide stronger local-defense flotillas for Hawaii, Alaska, Panama and our West Coast. Finally, the experimental fund provided in the present naval estimates should be at once used for the development of new types of small craft to support these local-defense flotillas—notably small, fast motor torpedo-boats, mine-layers, mine-sweepers, net-layers, and also escort vessels for the protection of merchant convoys. The convoy of our huge intercoastal traffic thru waters infested by enemy long-range submarines would certainly be a feature of any Pacific war, as would also the convoy of vessels engaged in the supply of our distant island bases.

In so enormous a water area as the Pacific, long-range patrol planes will play a great part, linking up our bases and patrolling the vast seas between them. We have 323 of these planes on hand or on order; the number will doubtless be increased out of the 1,000 additional planes provided for the navy. Other types will also be needed, such as scout planes for the cruisers, fighting planes and bombers for the carriers. One or two additional carriers may be required; experience with those now completing will be the best test of this.

So much for the Pacific area. There remains the Atlantic, where we must reckon on the possibility that Germany or Italy, or both, vitally in need as they are of raw materials, may attempt some form of Latin American adventure at a time when we are having trouble with Japan. The exact form which this might take it is needless to examine here; it is sufficient to observe that a mutual-defense pact imposes mutual obligations; if we are called upon we must be prepared to support our associates.

The German navy today has two battleships completing, three under construction; there are also three "pocket battleships," which are really heavily armed, long-range, fast armored cruisers; there are six cruisers ready, and five, plus two aircraft carriers, under construction, together with smaller craft. Italy has two battleships in commission, two more undergoing modernization, two new ones launched which may be ready late this year or early next, and two more projected. She has seven heavy cruisers, twelve light cruisers, and a strong force of flotilla craft.

This makes a formidable combined force; but it is going far indeed to assume that it could all be sent out of European waters. Germany could not afford to leave the Baltic a Soviet lake, nor could Italy denude the Mediterranean of naval defense. Of the total of thirteen battleships ultimately available to the two powers, it is difficult to see how more than half—say even—could ever be employed so far away from home. If we had five battleships in the Caribbean area, plus the proper proportion of other ships, the operations of such a force in South American waters would be impossible. This is not to say that we need sixteen battleships for the Pacific and five for the Atlantic. These proportions can be reduced because—and only because—we are in possession of the Panama Canal, giving us the inestimable military advantage of interior lines. If we have two battleships in the Atlantic with the Training Squadron, they can be reinforced by three from the Pacific within a reasonable time; and this will still leave us thirteen in the Pacific, a strength which can be attained for active service by quickly completing for sea such vessels as are undergoing overhaul.

It may be asked why an inferior force in the Atlantic will give us security while in the Pacific we need at least equality and preferably a 20 per cent margin. The answer is geographical. Any force menacing us in the Atlantic, or contemplating operations in South American waters, must in the first instance drive our fleet from the Caribbean Sea; otherwise our positions there will outflank any raid against our coast and will threaten the communications of any force moving into the South Atlantic. A European enemy would not have the vast reaches of the Pacific in which to maneuver for favorable position and opportunity; it must concentrate its effort on a single area. An attempt to conduct operations in South American waters without driving our fleet out of the Caribbean would be sheer madness.

Thus we require, not two fleets, but one, with its core a force of eighteen battleships, of which two or three may be in the Atlantic while the main force should for the present be concentrated in the Pacific. The Atlantic will also need a few cruisers, a squadron or two of destroyers, and very strong local-defense flotillas made up of submarines and of the special types to be developed by experiment. These should be stationed at New York, Norfolk and at Key West or one of the Caribbean bases.

As to battleship replacements, too great haste seems unwise. If, for example, Japan is not really building 43,000-ton ships, we will not find it sound policy to build such ships, which would have to be designed on rather unsatisfactory lines from a sea-keeping point of view to pass thru the Panama Canal. Also we might watch the possibility that Japan may (as suggested recently in the press and as predicted by a British naval authority, Sir Oscar Parkes, two years ago) be building fast armored cruisers armed with 12-inch guns; in this case—since such ships would be able to run away from our battleships and sink our cruisers, and would offer a most formidable menace to our commerce—we might have to convert some of our battleship funds into the building of small battle-cruisers which could run down and destroy this type of ship. The German pocket-battleships are the forerunners of this type. In scrapping older ships, also, we might well follow the lead of our potential enemies instead of anticipating it.

Our fleet is our primary defense instrument; it defends our shores, but its bases, essential to its operation, must be defended by the army. This is the army's No. 1 task. The present budget strength of the army is 12,590 officers and 165,000 enlisted men. The officer strength is to be built up to a total of 14,650 by means of annual increments. Behind the regular army is the National Guard, of which the authorized strength is to reach 210,000 next year. There are also some 110,000 reserve officers, for whom the principal source of increment is the R.O.T.C. at our colleges.

The size of our army does not need to be based on the size of foreign armies. It may be quite otherwise estimated. First, the necessary garrisons to make Hawaii and Panama secure. Hawaii must be able to defend itself against the heaviest possible attack, in the absence of the fleet, for a period of time sufficient for the fleet to reach it from the Atlantic Seaboard—if for any reason the fleet should be called there. Panama must be insured against surprise above all things; the units here should be at full war strength, and there should be powerful long-range bombing planes to deal with any possible attempt to establish an enemy base in neutral territory nearby. The Hawaiian garrison (18,000) is probably sufficient for immediate needs; that at Panama (13,000) requires a modest increase, say 2,000 men. A beginning should be made in erecting and manning harbor defenses at Guantanamo and an Aleutian base; 1,000 men each, mostly coast artillery, would be needed. Further development could be left to experience.

The continental United States requires first of all adequate harbor defenses, to protect our fleet bases and also to prevent an enemy fleet entering any of our principal commercial harbors, say in the ocean in which our fleet was not present at the moment; either to establish a base there or to destroy the harbor works and perhaps lay one of our cities under bombardment. Adequate harbor defenses release the mobile land, air and sea forces from responsibility for the defense of these positions, to perform their true functions; thus it is a highly economical program from a military point of view, and also from the view of the treasury, as such defenses, once constructed, are inexpensive to maintain. A five-year program for the modernization of the defenses of the Pacific Coast harbors and those of Hawaii and Panama was determined upon by a congressional committee which visited those places in 1936; the cost, $15,000,000 over a period of five years. Similar modernization of the Atlantic defenses is estimated at $34,000,000.

The air corps ought not to be scattered in little detachments around our coast (save a few planes for artillery spotting), but held in concentrated force to be hurled at any threatened point; its characteristics of range, speed and flexibility support this policy. The General Headquarters Air Force is a step in this direction. The present objective is for about 2,400 planes in operating squadrons; it is doubtful whether it would be economical to build much beyond this point at present. Pilots and trained enlisted personnel take much longer to produce than planes; the air corps in the continental United States ought to have a total of 20,000 officers and men. Air attacks on our great cities are impossible unless the enemy can bring his planes in carriers (which is a matter for the navy to deal with in the first place, and our air corps in the second) or unless he can establish a shore air-base within flying range. If this base is to be established on our own coasts, it comes within the discussion below of

attempted invasion; if on the coast of one of our neighbors, it must be within range of our own air corps, and
its communications are open to interruption by our fleet.
Finally, the suggested increase in anti-aircraft artillery
will provide local defense. Unless a successful invasion
is accomplished, our cities need at worst fear nothing
more than a "tip-and-run" air raid.

NAVAL ESTABLISHMENT [6]

1. *Naval Expansion.* The Naval Expansion Act,
which provoked the sharpest debates of the session on
foreign policy and national defense, was introduced January 28 and finally signed by the President on May 17.
House approval came on March 21, by a vote of 294 to
100, after a militant minority of the House Naval Affairs
Committee carried their fight against the bill to the House
floor. In the Senate a well-organized opposition sub-
jected the bill to scathing attack, but at the end of a
fortnight's debate their persistent questions as to what
naval expansion was for remained unanswered.

The Expansion Act, designed to raise naval strength
approximately 20 per cent above existing authorizations,
adds 46 new warships and 26 auxiliaries, raising the limit
to 272 "under-age" ships of 1,557,480 tons. Since the
navy's present tonnage in modern "under-age" vessels
is only about 919,355 tons, the practical effect of the act
is not to increase fleet strength by 20 per cent but to
authorize a navy between 50 and 60 per cent stronger
than the *fleet in commission* today. Moreover, since
expiration of the naval treaties the government is under
no obligation to scrap older vessels. Tho designated
"over-age" and "obsolescent" such vessels are still considered useful to the navy, even tho less efficient in fighting strength. Present replacements to the fleet are there-

[6] *Washington Information Service of the National Peace Conference.*
1:5-8. June 1, 1938.

fore actually additions to the navy's force, and the United States fleet—given retention of all fifteen capital ships now in commission, and completion of the nine now authorized, appropriated for or building—will have some twenty-three battleships in commission by 1943-44. The regular appropriations bill provides for the laying down of two battleships and the carrying forward of work on a second pair; the naval expansion bill authorizes three additional capital ships, and the President's supplementary naval estimates—to be carried in the second deficiency appropriations bill—authorizes two more.

Cost of the naval expansion authorized in the big-navy bill is estimated by the administration at $1,156,-000,000. Observers point out, however, that this estimate is based upon present building costs, that by the time the program is carried out increased costs may more than double this figure. The fact that bids submitted upon the Maritime Commission's fleet of new tankers were higher than the Commission's own estimates by some 50 per cent—according to the testimony of former chairman Joseph P. Kennedy—goes far to substantiate this claim.

2. *Vessel Strength.* Vessels now building, appropriated for under the regular 1939 bill, authorized under the naval expansion bill, and to be appropriated for under the pending second deficiency appropriations bill are shown in table 1.

In addition, the Naval Expansion Act, by setting the limit of "useful naval airplanes" at "not less than three thousand," authorized the building of at least 950 airplanes; the construction of small experimental vessels to the sum of $15,000,000; and the building of a rigid airship at $3,000,000. Funds for beginning the airship are expected to be provided in the second deficiency appropriations act, as well as funds for constructing an indefinite number of the experimental torpedo vessels. The second deficiency is also expected to provide funds

TABLE 1

PROPOSED VESSEL STRENGTH

Type of Vessel	Now Building		Appropriated for, regular 1939 apropriations act		Appropriated for in pending second deficiency appropriations act, requested in supplementary naval estimates		Authorized under naval expansion bill		Grand Total	
	No.	Tonnage	No.	Tonnage	No.	Tonnage	No.	Tonnage	No.	Tonnage
Battleships	2	70,000	2	70,000	2	70,000	3	135,000	9	345,000
Aircraft Carriers	2	34,600					2	40,000	4	74,600
Cruisers (a)	1	10,000							1	10,000
Cruisers (b)	7	17,000	2	10,000			9	68,754	18	95,754
Destroyers	36	56,200	8	12,000			23	38,000	67	104,200
Submarines	15	21,740	6	8,130			9	13,658	30	43,528
Small auxiliaries	2	18,250	4	18,750			26	133,650	32	170,380
Totals	65	280,790	22	118,880	2	70,000	72	429,062	161	843,462

for beginning construction upon one aircraft carrier, two light cruisers, ten auxiliary vessels, and nine 4-engine naval patrol planes—all authorized under the naval expansion act.

3. *Naval Appropriations Act for 1939.* Most significant features of the regular appropriations act for 1938-39 were the increases in items for improving the preparedness of the existing fleet. The fund for new construction exceeded last year's appropriation by $13,700,-000, the naval supply account fund was increased by $7,000,000, the fund for shore station improvement and expansion by $6,242,074, and the item for fleet improvement by $4,281,800. Under the increases in personnel the addition of over 5,500 recruits will bring the navy to "treaty" strength of 111,000 men by the end of next year—two years ahead of schedule. Marine enlisted personnel will be raised by 1,000.

TABLE 2

UNITED STATES MILITARY AND NAVAL EXPENDITURES, 1930-1939
(*In Thousands of Dollars*)

	Fiscal Year	War Department	Navy Department	Total
	1913	202,128	133,262	335,390
	1930	327,363	373,905	701,268
	1931	345,274	353,902	699,176
	1932	344,610	357,820	702,430
	1933	298,417	349,732	648,149
Incl. Emergency Expenditures	1934	243,329	297,188	540,517
	1935	273,485	438,001	711,486
	1936	382,654	530,702	913,356
	1937	374,260	550,648	924,908
	1938	433,762 [1]	558,431 [2]	992,193 [3]
	1939	430,814	580,047	1,010,861 [4]

[1] Compiled from Summary Budget Statements, 1930 thru 1939.
[2] Budget estimate.
[3] Includes budget estimate of $23,624,280 for Public Works expenditure, War Department, and $7,645,610, Navy Department, not listed in regular budget.
[4] Includes budget estimate of $11,547,856 for Public Works expenditures, War Department, and $8,000,000, Navy Department not listed in regular budget.

The appropriation of $44,170,000 for construction of new airplanes will, according to the prediction of the House appropriations committee, provide the navy with 1,870 useful planes by the end of the fiscal year—forty planes short of the 1941 objective of 1,910 planes.

Besides appropriating $119,641,050 for carrying forward work on 72 warships and two auxiliaries the measure provides $18,422,100 for beginning construction on 18 warships and four auxiliaries, all of which are authorized under the Vinson-Trammel Act of 1934.

United States military and naval expenditures from 1930 thru the estimates for the current year, preceded by the figure for 1913, are shown in table 2.

BRIEF EXCERPTS

Today it is a commonplace that civilization sits on a powder keg, and already the time fuse may have been set for the explosion. *A. D. Hutton. Rotarian. O. '37. p. 7.*

We cannot expect other nations to accept the British formula that our armaments promote peace while theirs promote war; but we can perhaps get them to agree that the mad competition in armaments, or rearmaments, is leading to insolvency and general ruin. *Francis W. Hirst. Contemporary Review. Je '38. p. 646.*

Europe will leave no stone unturned to convince the United States once more that the issue is purely one of making the world safe for democracy, of securing peace, or anything that makes good reading as far as the American public is concerned. *Pierre J. Huss, Central European Manager for International News Service. Newsdom. Je. 19, '37. p. 3.*

There can be no real security for any nation, industrial or agricultural, and consequently there can be no lasting international peace or stability, until nations can secure for themselves access, free from prohibitive nationalistic barriers, first to necessary raw materials and foodstuffs, and second to foreign markets. *Francis Bowes Sayre. New York Times Magazine. N.* 22, '36. *p.* 26.

How many realize that in asking for preponderant force as an instrument of defense to be used in the old way we arc beginning with a denial of right—denial to the weaker state of that right of defense by superior power which we claim for ourselves, the denial to the weaker of that right of judgment which we claim for ourselves? *Normal Angell. Adult Education. D.* '37. *p.* 152.

The momentous question is—whether this and other peaceful nations fervently attached to the principles which underlie international order shall work unceasingly—singly or in cooperation with each other, as circumstances, their traditional policies, and practices, and their enlightened self-interest may dictate—to promote and preserve law, order, morality and justice as the unshakeable bases of civilised international relations. *Cordell Hull, Secretary of State. Landmark. Ap.* '38. *p.* 193.

The challenge to those who would have our nation defended adequately is to see the problem in all its aspects, to make the effort to know all the pertinent facts, and to make choices based upon a realistic balancing of ultimate advantages against costs and risks. Without this attitude and this effort we constantly run the risk of drifting into crises without having the power to decide how they shall be resolved. *Esther Caukin Brunauer. National Defense. Womans Press.* N.Y. '37. *p.* 51.

Protestation of peace and the desire for peace, however sincere, do not guarantee the self-denying spirit necessary for the maintenance of peace, even at the cost of national sacrifice. If any statesman should think that the apparatus to ensure peace is, as yet, insufficiently organized, we advise them to devote to this purpose as much energy and as much money as is now being expended on the armaments of the various countries. *Letter of Psychiatrists to the Statesmen of the World. League of Nations. O.* '35.

Some there are who find a fallacy in the whole idea of disarmament. Man fought, they hold, when he had only fists for weapons, and to fight he will continue no matter how he be disarmed. This idea was reduced to an epigram by the Paris correspondent of the New York *Times,* who summarized the conference as follows: "Americans believe that if Cain had not had a club he would not have killed Abel. Europeans believe that if Abel had had a club he would not have been killed. *Louis Martin Sears. A History of American Foreign Relations. Thomas Y. Crowell Co.* N.Y. '36. *p.* 590.

Battleships come at $50,000,000 apiece; four of them make $200,000,000, which offhand sounds like militarism gone mad. But—aside from the fact that it is a criminal waste to spend any money whatever on battleships—it is not so bad as it seems. Before the four new ships are ready, in 1940-41, the navy will have to begin scrapping its existing fleet. England is in a similar fix, and if past experience is a guide, we may confidently expect that the United States and England will be ready with a noble offer of partial naval disarmament about 1940-41. *New Republic. Ja.* 5, '38. *p.* 253.

There exist today five treaties for the prevention of war, to which the United States has subscribed. At the last Pan-American Conference, held in Montevideo in 1933, a resolution was adopted urging all member governments to ratify these engagements, but few have done so.

These treaties, which together are supposed to supply complete apparatus for determining all disputes by pacific means, are the Pact of Paris, the Argentine Anti-War pact, the Gondra pact, the Inter-American Conciliation treaty and the Inter-American Arbitration treaty. *H. B. Hinton. New York Times. F.* 23, '36. *Sec.* 4 *p.* 7.

A wholesome sign appears in the recent announcement of the Massachusetts Institute of Technology that it will exempt conscientious objectors to military training from the requirement of such training for a degree (provided their reasons are approved by the faculty), if they substitute therefor certain studies in international law and the history of arbitration and diplomacy; tho the details of the alternative courses have not yet been definitely determined. This, if carried out in good faith, is a substantial advance. Nothing is more effective toward international understanding than informed intelligence about "how we got that way." *John Palmer Gavit. Survey Graphic. Ap.* '37. *p.* 222.

I do not think leadership lies along the path of isolation. I think it lies along the path of farsightedness, study, understanding, sympathy, but also of decision as to what we think the principle of world behavior should be.

We should be willing to pay a large price for peace but there is one price I hope we shall never pay. I hope we shall always be a nation that can decide between right and wrong. I hope we shall never go to war but more than that, I hope we shall never compromise with our principles. *Mrs. Franklin D. Roosevelt. New York Times. Ja.* 20, '38. *p.* 8.

While military arms were grounded on Armistice Day nineteen years ago, economic arms were multiplied many times in number and in destructive power. Where freedom was expected to rule, compulsion and regimentation have taken its place. Instead of unselfish human service on the highest plane of economic and moral excellence, we are confronted with a world of nations every one of which is engaged in the process of economic self-destruction by policies which for the moment it regards as nationally advantageous. Lack of understanding, lack of foresight, lack of moral sense, are paralyzing the world and inviting the rule of force which, when it comes. quickly becomes the rule of armed force. *Nicholas Murray Butler. Vital Speeches. D.* 1, '37. *p.* 117.

The non-intervention policy that has been pursued by the United States in its external relations has been translated, in military terms, into an establishment that would be strictly defensive were it not for the size and, to a lesser extent, the composition of its naval forces. The defensive task in the Pacific consists in protecting the country, its territories and commerce against invasion, raids and interference. To this end an imposing navy with 110,000 officers and men and 17,000 marines, representing an investment exceeding $3,000,000,000, is based upon the West Coast, with Hawaii as a pivoting point, its wings stretching from Alaska to Panama, and outposts at Guam and Manila, points which have been provided with coastal fortifications and aerial and military protection. *Alexander Kirafly. Pacific Affairs. Je. '38. p. 208.*

Even the smaller nations are making frantic efforts to provide themselves with the most modern weapons of destruction. Unless a halt is soon called to this "Dance of Death" it seems inevitable that some of the dancers will decide to use these weapons, probably to avert an internal conflagration.

To avert this danger, whose reality is, self-evident, there seems nothing save the twofold possibility that the pacifist powers will be so strong and united that the "have-nots" will be afraid of attacking them, or so far-sighted and intelligent as to satisfy the legitimate aims and aspirations of the "have-nots" by amicable compromise. *Walter Duranty. New York Times Magazine. Je. 13, '37. p. 16.*

No one needs to be told today that for twenty years we have enjoyed a false security, based on a covenant we have failed to adhere to and which other governments no longer depend on. If they did they would not be arming to their eyebrows while every last one claims to be working for peace. Hitler marches into Austria as he did into the Rhineland in the name of peace. Mussolini summmons 9,000,000 unknown soldiers for an oratorical parade as guardians of the peace. Japan does not declare war; she is bringing peace to China. In all the forges, factories, laboratories, shipyards and training fields of the world we are witnessing the *reductio ad absurdam* of the argument for military preparedness. The battered old earth has become one vast armament works for the manufacturing of peace. *Anne O'Hare McCormick. America's Town Meeting of the Air. Bulletin. Ap. 11, '38. p. 8.*

Are measures of armament to be determined in fact by the civil branches of the federal government?

Or are they to be dictated by the navy bureaucracy, in particular the General Board of the Navy, supported by a powerful array of active cupidity—an array that includes: place-holders eager for salary increases, promotions, and more imposing jobs; armor-plate manufacturers; munition-makers; merchant-marine promoters, as providers of naval auxiliaries; navy-yard communities dependent on naval construction for employment and profits; labor interests, looking for high wages; real estate boomers; the jingo press, making money out of rabble-rousing; hyphenates, bent on war with England; the anti-Japanese and the pro-Chinese hunting trouble in the Pacific; merchants selling military and naval supplies—working openly or under cover, with millions of dollars at stake in naval expenditures and huge funds available for propaganda? *Charles A. Beard. Navy: Defense or Portent. Harper & Bros. N.Y. '32. p.* 5-6.

The peace system has broken down in theory as well as in practice. Later events, like the conquest of Ethiopia and Japan's new war in China, have only revealed and verified the melancholy fact that there is no peace system left. The nations are proceeding in their independent ways to make alliances and to prepare their own defenses in precisely the same fashion as before any collective peace structure was set up.

The disillusionment is complete—no less so in Europe and Asia than in the United States. It takes the form of utter skepticism with respect to the major premise upon which all peace plans have been built—namely, that governments will honor their plighted word to act for peace quite apart from their own national or imperial interests. It is a cynical conclusion. But it is realistic and indubitable. *Christian Century. S.* 15, '37. *p.* 1129.

It seems clear that the disarmament approach to security was an over-simplification of the problem. Because the idea was easy and rational, it has had great public support. But the efforts at disarmament have now proved that no single-minded approach to peace is sufficient. It is impossible to isolate the problem of disarmament from the problem of substitutes for armaments and until such time as the nations of the world are willing to discuss, along with the amount of armaments, the uses for which they are devised, there can be no relief for the citizen from armament taxes and from fears created by the existence of armaments.

Originally a part of the collective system to prevent war, the disarmament program as it has evolved into a rearmament program is now a direct denial of the theory of collective security. Every time one nation asserts that its armaments must be equal to or bigger than those of another nation, a complete lack of confidence in the collective theory is shown. *Louise Leonard Wright. Toward a Collective Peace System. National League of Women Voters. Wash. D.C. '37. p. 24-5.*

Initiation of the new naval race came from nations classified as the "have-nots" which have experienced resurgent military nationalism in the last five years. For them, naval rearmament was part and parcel of the general rearmament incidental to demands for recognition as major powers.

The one incident which, more than any other, started the race was Germany's launching of the 10,000-ton "pocket" battleship *Deutschland* in 1931. France immediately countered by building two battleships of 26,500 tons each. Italy followed by announcing two 35,000-ton battleships and France countered again with two 35,000-tonners.

Meanwhile, Germany built two more "pocket" battleships and is planning two full-sized units of the 35,000-ton category, to which France says she will add three more for a total of five. No longer bound by the fourteen-year holiday on "battle-wagons," Japan has drafted plans for four new monsters, while the United States and Britain are calling for two each. *Literary Digest. Ja. 9, '37. p. 6.*

On February 11 the chairman of the House Naval Committee, Congressman Carl Vinson, announced that there would be written into the pending bill which authorizes construction of Mr. Roosevelt's desired super-navy a special section officially stating the governmental policy which the United States navy is to serve. This official declaration we quote verbatim:

It is declared to be the fundamental naval policy of the United States to maintain an adequate navy in sufficient strength to guard the continental United States by affording naval protection to the coastline, in both oceans at one and the same time; to protect the Panama Canal, Alaska, Hawaii and our insular possessions; to protect our commerce and citizens abroad; to maintain a navy in sufficient strength to guarantee our national security, but not for aggression; to insure our national integrity, and to support our national policies.

It is further declared to be the policy of the United States that an adequate naval defense means not only the protection of our continental coastline, the Canal Zone, Alaska, Hawaii and our insular possessions, but also a defense that will keep any potential enemy away from our shores.

Christian Century. F. 23, '38. p. 230-1.

In American foreign policy, at least since the days of Woodrow Wilson, two ideas have clashed. They are clashing now as the United States looks out upon a world torn by war and threatened by more war.

On one hand are the isolationists who would have the United States follow the traditional policy of avoiding "entangling alliances," who believe that American destiny is at home and that naval and military armament should be predicated on defense of the coast and near-by waters.

Opposed to this way of thinking are those who would cooperate with foreign nations in the cause of international peace, who believe that a nation cannot have peace without doing something to earn it. This group, at first identified with support of the League of Nations, has more recently advocated, or at least inclined toward, understandings with powers that share American hostility toward fascist aggression. A strong navy and efficient army are demanded for national defense as a warning to aggressive nations. That warning, it has been said, could in itself tend to halt the fascist march. *Why a Big Navy? New York Times. F.* 13, '38. *Sec.* 4, *p.* 1.

The situation in the world is one of delicate balance —the forces of peace and the forces of war. I do not know which is going to win out but over here on this side of the world is the greatest and strongest power, having vast economic and financial resources. If we use our powers in the proper way, if we join them with the other forces in the world working for peace, if we work out a program and say to the dictatorships: "We realize the fundamental maladjustment. We will help you solve your problems. Let us do something about tariffs and debts. You can disarm and do no further acts of aggression." If we would show courage and take that responsibility, then I feel this world war is going to be averted and that we will get thru this transitional period. We will enter a new state of stability marked by a greater degree of security for our children, a greater degree of social justice, a greater degree of peace. I do not know whether we are going to swing the balance toward catastrophe or the other way toward peace and social justice. But I am inclined to think America holds a key and that the future of civilization lies in our hands. *Raymond Leslie Buell. National Education Association. Proceedings,* 1937. *p.* 134.

In view of the uncertainties abroad, it is possible that a clear statement of policy at this time would be very difficult. But certain major points of policy should certainly be explained without further delay. It appears that we will defend a line of approximately 10,000 miles extending from the Aleutian Islands to Hawaii to Samoa to Panama and up thru the Caribbean to the Virgin Islands and thence to the coast of Maine. But what about the Philippines? Furthermore, Representative Vinson has announced that we must be prepared to enforce the Monroe Doctrine. Are we going to defend the 10,000-mile line, or are we going to defend the whole of Central and South America? It might also be well to emphasize the fact that some people are convinced, despite Admiral Leahy's disarming statements, that a big navy is called for in order to take summary action against "aggressor" nations and that, in particular, if American rights continue to be violated by the Japanese, the major part of our enlarged fleet will suddenly disappear one fine morning under forced draft for Tokyo. And who shall say that their surmise is correct? *Commonweal. F.* 18, '38. *p.* 450.

Principal Causes Of War
   1.   Economic
        a.   Trade
                Struggle for markets
                Unfair competition
                Shipping rivalry
                International bankers
                Monopolies, cartels
                Munitions makers
        b.   Self-preservation
                Low food supply
                Excessive population

    c.   Imperialism
        Struggle for colonies
        Protecting markets
        Quest of raw materials
        Guarding strategic areas
        Exploiting natives
        Financing development of colonies

2. Political
    a.   Intrigue, propaganda
        Communism
        Naziism
        Fascism
        British Foreign Office
    b.   Domestic disorders
    c.   Armaments race
    d.   Aggressive diplomacy
    e.   Treaties, alliances for balance of power
    f.   Disgruntled minorities
    g.   Honor, prestige, revenge

3. Other causes
    a.   Plunder
    b.   Jingoism
    c.   Conquest
    d.   Dynastic ambitions
    e.   Nationalism
    f.   Racial rivalry
    g.   Religious intolerance
    h.   Self-determination

Newsdom. F. 19, '38. *p.* 8.

I do not believe that a modern city can exist without a police force to repress crime or without courts to enforce contracts. No more do I believe that the modern world can exist without agencies of order and justice. We have tried and the results are before us. Gangster nations have broken loose and declared their intentions to seize what they want.

For America to imagine it can stand aloof in this crisis is as if Brooklyn should retire behind the East River and refuse to concern itself with anarchy existing in New York. To exactly the extent that Brooklyn kept order and prosperity, it would become the object of the desires of the New York gangsters, and would have to arm to protect itself.

If democracy is to survive this crisis, the democratic nations must organize at once and declare their intention to enforce law and order thruout civilization. Gangster nations planning raids must know not merely that they will be boycotted completely, but that if this does not suffice, an international army and navy will overthrow their dictators, hold a plebiscite, and establish a new government by popular consent.

In the circumstances existing, this program means a call to all men of good-will to stop fascism. In my opinion it will not mean war. It will mean organization, education, and a firm demand on the gangster states. The people of those states want peace and order as much as the rest of us, and will not fight long against a program of international justice. *Upton Sinclair. The Nation. Ap. 2, '38. p. 377.*

Anxious statesmen undoubtedly consider that by rearming greater security is being obtained. Yet it is a paradox that, if all states increase their armaments in roughly the same proportion, the relative security of each has not changed at all, except possibly for the worse. Dictators are rearming because they desire to altar the balance of armaments to their advantage and then to use war or threat of it as an instrument of policy. But this only calls forth fresh efforts in turn from the countries that believe themselves menaced, and so the race goes on. A sudden spurt may give a temporary advantage and, as the pressure increases, this may be used as the moment to strike.

Rearming has become a psychological condition. We are back to the law of the jungle where every country is trying to make itself as safe as armaments can make it and is terrified of being left behind in the race. Small countries like Holland or Switzerland can make no conceivable addition to their armed strength that would make the difference between victory and defeat or deter a great power from invading them, if it were thought worth while. Yet they are determined to do their best to make the aggressor pay as great a price as possible. Indeed, to go further, are the U.S.S.R. or Germany a whit more secure for the prodigious efforts that they have made? Financially they are certainly much poorer and each is honestly afraid of the other. *A. C. Temperley. Review of Reviews. Mr. '37. p. 76-7. Quoted from World Review.*

After we have provided adequate defense for our nation, as we shall do, the problems of democracy remain. The healing is not to be found in armaments, but in bringing contentment, happiness and prosperity to the harried, confused and discouraged citizen.

There is greater danger to our democracy in that vast army of unemployed encamped in every city, town and village thruout the land, in that 50,000,000 men, women and children living in constant sight of the poverty line, poorly clad and poorly fed, in the hundreds of thousands, with the number increasing every year, of malformed and rickety children, of the 5,000,000 girls and boys who leave colleges and universities, finding no avenue in which to engage their energies, their genius, more danger here by far than in any fleet of battleships which any nation or group of nations may choose to send against us.

I care not what flag floats over a people, what their traditions as to liberty may be, how well their institutions of government express the aspirations and hopes of a people, crushing taxes and hunger and disease and broken families will in time undermine and destroy all these things. *Senator William E. Borah. New York Times. Mr. 29, '38. p. 3.*

If anything has been demonstrated in the last months, it is that you cannot be at the same time a pacifist and an international reformer.

The British Labor party has got itself into a most serious dilemma by this confusion of thought. It wanted collective security, with sanctions to enforce peace on the wicked aggressor, and it wanted at the same time British disarmament. The result was that Britain got out on a limb from which she had to retreat with considerable ignominy. And the cause of international peace was certainly ill served. Now Britain has gone into reverse. She is arming with tremendous speed, while the country goes thru a revulsion of feeling, moving to the position that Britain from now on will fight exclusively for British interests. First you had holy crusaders, plus pacifism; now you have armament, plus pacifism. Neither seems a very good combination.

Holland built a crack army, and when the war broke out mobilized it and kept it mobilized at great expense during the entire hostilities. It was perfectly clear that any one who invaded Holland would not have an easy time of it, small tho the country was. But having done this, Holland took more blows on the chin, more insults to national pride, more interference and more suffering than is easily imaginable. She was between two fires. *Dorothy Thompson. New York Times. S. 11, '36. p. 23.*

There seems to be no question that the Japanese occupation of Manchuria in 1931 was the beginning of a chain of events that led directly to much of the present difficulty in which the world finds itself. Four years later Germany announced its adoption of rearmament and conscription in violation of the treaty of Versailles, and the next year came the occupation of the Rhineland. I do not pass judgment on these events. There were circumstances in both instances that to outsiders might seem to be extenuating, and to the German people completely justifying what was done.

In the same year with German conscription came the Italian attack upon Ethiopia, which was adjudged by the League of Nations a violation of the League covenant which Italy had signed. This was followed by armed intervention in the civil war in Spain, and finally by the Japanese invasion of China. I need hardly remind you that the resulting trouble in the Mediterranean and the destruction of life and property in China not only have affected American interests, but have contributed to world demoralization.

It is a fair inference that this chain of events was in direct consequence of the success of Japan in setting up the state of Manchukuo without effective objection from the democratic powers. Each incident has had repercussions on the world situation until today there is less reliance upon the sanctity of treaties, less trust in international good faith, less confidence upon which to build lasting prosperity, than there has been for a long time. *Harry H. Woodring, Secretary of War. Address, May 5, 1938. Mimeo. p. 3.*

Taking into account the recent tendencies in American foreign policy it should be possible to draw up a tentative list of national interests which the army and navy might be called upon to defend. Such a list, submitted with all due reservations, might include the following:

1. Defense of the continental United States.
2. Defense of overseas possessions.

3. Control of the seas adjacent to the continental United States.

4. Defense of the Monroe Doctrine interpreted as a continental understanding in accord with agreements reached at the last Pan-American Conference.

5. Protection of American foreign commerce and defense of "neutral rights" under certain conditions.

6. Maintenance of the open door in China.

7. Preservation of the territorial integrity of China.

Other less tangible interests might be added:

8. Preservation of American institutions and democracy.

9. Diplomatic support of other democratic nations against "aggressive" dictatorships.

10. Preservation of the "sanctity of treaties" and the "rule of law" in international relations.

Objections to this list will vary with the political and social philosophy of the individual or the group. Those who believe that a high standard of living under the capitalist system demands expanding foreign markets will insist that strong defense of American economic interests is essential to the welfare of this nation. Those who believe that a high standard of living can be achieved by internal adjustments brought about without violence will eliminate several items as not essential to the life of the nation. Since there is no way of resolving these conflicting philosophies, perhaps the pragmatic list may be allowed to stand. *William T. Stone. Peace or War; a Conference. Univ. of Minnesota Press. Minneapolis. Je. '37. p. 158.*

The basic cause of every great war has always been and ever will be economic. Wanting more of this world's goods than they have and oftentimes actually requiring more if they are to increase and multiply or even merely live, people exert tremendous pressures on their governments to provide what the people believe they require. Since governments came into being and remain in being solely for the benefit of the people governed, they must provide what their people require or face overthrow by revolution. To almost any government war is preferable to revolution, and is especially preferable if there is a chance of winning, since a war for their personal advantage tends to bind a people to their government. Hence governments are often forced to take a chance and, under the pressure of their people to provide them a better living, commit the overt act the economic demand calls for and that so often is cited as the cause of the war that follows.

The overt acts that open wars are rather similar in nature. We find them stated in terms such as the selfish seeking of territory for self-aggrandizement or world dominion, as the money-making schemes of capitalists or munition makers; and so forth and so on. However, when we try to prevent thru seeking to end these overt acts said to be the causes of war we get nowhere because those acts are a result of the cause and not the cause itself.

If we are ever to prevent war we must do it in quite other ways than those frequently advocated. Knowing the basic cause is always an economic demand of a people, we must prevent such demands or else face the consequences. But is it possible ever to prevent such demands when to do so all peoples must feel satisfied with what they have; must be content to live on only what is now theirs; must believe the present distribution of world's goods among nations is just; and must agree that they have no right to increase and multiply beyond what their countries can now care for. If we can persuade all peoples to accept those beliefs

the one great basic cause of war will be gone. But
until we can so persuade them war will ever be with us.
*Rear Admiral Harris Laning. United States Senate.
Committee on Naval Affairs. Naval Expansion program;
Hearings on H.R.9218. 75th Cong. 1st Sess. Ap.* 4-13,
'38. *p.* 408.

Steady pressure for a bigger navy dates back to the
1880's when a struggle developed between American,
British and German interests for commercial advantages.
In 1895, the demand was stimulated by a situation that
grew out of our dispute with England over its demands
upon Venezuela.

The annexation of Hawaii, the acquisition of Puerto
Rico and the Philippines, and the establishment of a
protectorate over Cuba and the construction of the
Panama Canal, provided further reasons for naval expansion.

The influence of Theodore Roosevelt on the policies of
the government was decisive. In a message to Congress,
December 4, 1904, he urged a great navy to guard overseas possessions, and to protect the nation's commerce.
During Roosevelt's term as President, the number of
ships in the navy was nearly doubled and the size of the
ships constructed greatly increased.

Commercial and financial interests were quick to
back up the big navy policy. In 1902, the Navy League
of the United States was organized on the initiative of
the New York Chapter of the Naval Order of the United
States. The early statements of the League declared
it was founded "on the same lines as the Leagues of
Germany, Great Britain and France," and credited the
German Navy League, then five years old, as being the
chief influence in the development of the German Navy.
The purpose of the Navy League was said to be "to
inculcate among all the people of every section of our
common country a better understanding of the urgent
need of naval expansion."

Among the Navy League's list of founders were J. Pierpont Morgan, General B. F. Tracy, George Westinghouse, Colonel John Jacob Astor, Charles M. Schwab, Colonel John J. McCook, and Harry Payne Whitney, and the Midvale Steel Company.

In a speech before Congress on December 15, 1915, Representative Clyde Tavenner, of Illinois, pointed out that the majority of the directors of the Navy League, year by year, were directly or thru interlocking directorates connected with manufacturers who would profit from the success of the Navy League's propaganda for increased armaments. *Florence Brewer Boeckel. What Is Our National Defense Policy. National Council for Prevention of War. Wash. D.C. Ja.* 1, '37. *p.* 9-11.

It is no longer news that the world is spending more for armaments today than it was in 1914: we all got used to that fact some time back. Yet few of us realize how much more is being spent for guns and airplanes now, and most of us would be surprised and shocked to know the truth. Francis Williams, financial editor of the British Labor Party's newspaper, the *Daily Herald,* has gathered some figures on the subject which make anything but soothing reading. He finds that, between them, the United States, Britain, France, Germany, Italy, Japan and Russia spent roughly $2,200,000,000 for arms in 1914: their combined arms bill today he estimates at well over $11,000,000,000. The largest increase has, of course, been Germany's, rising from approximately $470,000,000 in 1914 to nearly $4,700,000,000 in 1936. Next comes Russia, with an expenditure of about $2,950,000,000 in 1936 as against $450,000,000 in 1914. The third largest arms bill for last year went to the United States: over $1,000,000,000, to be compared with $250,000,000 in the year of the outbreak of the World war. France spent $350,000,000 in 1914, and plans to spend over $900,000,00 in 1937. Britain's current outgo for armaments is $800,000,000; in 1914 it was $380,000,000. Italy has increased her arms budget from $180,000,000 to $750,000,000, and Japan's has jumped from $95,000,000 to $300,000,000. Mr. Williams warns that the difficulties of conversion make both the Russian and the German figures appear somewhat larger than, in terms of domestic purchasing power, they actually are, and, because Japan's standards of living are so low, the Japanese figures appear abnormally low. But, on the other hand, says Mr. Williams:

By comparing the amounts spent on arms in the various countries with their populations, it can be seen how enormously over-armed Germany is and how the Russian figure, tho large, is dwarfed when it is realized that she has a much longer frontier to defend.

Germany has 11.8 per cent of the total population of these seven powers, but 41 per cent of their combined arms bill is spent by her. Russia, with 29.8 per cent of the population, spends 26 per cent of the total arms bill.

The United States with 22.5 per cent of the population spends 8.8 per cent of the arms bill; Japan has 12.3 per cent of population and spends 2.6 per cent of the arms bill; Britain has 8.3 per cent of the population and spends 7 per cent of the arms bill; France has 7.4 per cent of the population and spends 8.1 per cent of the arms bill; Italy has 7.8 per cent of the population and spends 6.6 per cent of the arms bill.

Living Age. Ja. '37. p. 382-3.

Are these millions, now to be poured out at the rate of a billion a year, actually for defense? Or is a large part of such huge appropriations going for purposes which have no connection with genuine defense or for armaments which would prove useless in the day of battle? Are the taxpayers getting value received for their money? Or is Mr. Roosevelt using his enormous influence over Congress to give a group of swivel-chair admirals and generals an opportunity to go on a spending spree which, when it is finished, will leave this nation actually no more secure against attack than it now is? Is the President, in almost doubling defense expenditures within a single term, doubling the ability of our armed forces to repulse the invasion of a foreign foe? Or is he throwing these hundreds of millions down a sewer?

We do believe that this new budget, with its astronomical defense figures, makes it in order to ask certain simple but relevant questions. We waive for the present our objections to the whole military theory that national security lies in armed preparedness. We approach the issue now on the assumptions which have governed Mr. Roosevelt, the generals and the admirals in making up these budget figures. And we insist that the hard-pressed taxpayer has a right to ask: What is this billion dollars going to buy? How much of it is going to be thrown away?

Is it possible for army and navy establishments to spend money automatically, but uselessly, for ends which—speaking now from the professional military and naval point of view—have become obsolete? It is not only possible; it happens all the time. A good many Americans are at present reading the latest book by England's most distinguished military critic, Captain B. H. Liddell Hart. Captain Hart's book, *The War in Outline,* is essentially a demonstration of the incompetency of the high command of every nation engaged in the World war. "There is over two thousand years of experience to tell us," says Captain Hart, "that the only thing harder than getting a new idea into the military mind is to get an old one out." During the war, Captain Hart proves, the high command in every fighting nation insisted on pouring out money—and what was worse, men—in fruitless ways just because professional traditions handed down from the days of Clausewitz a century before approved, and opposing with equal doggedness the introduction of means and methods of fighting which would have saved hundreds of thousands of lives and brought a decision years earlier. "The tale," says

Captain Hart, "would be incredible were it not established fact." *Christian Century.* F. 10, '37. *p.* 175-6.

In making my classification I have not included two extreme points of view. On the one hand I have discarded those who advocate an attitude of complete resignation and inaction in the face of forceful aggression affecting even our domestic vital interests. I cannot seriously believe that even if 99 per cent of our population solemnly signed Aldous Huxley pledges never to go to war for any purpose, self defense included, their declared submission could survive up to the point where the first foreign bombs started demolishing our coast cities.

On the other hand, the group which would have us go to war for conquest, to extend our vital interests, without provocation from abroad, seems also to merit no recognition at this time.

Perhaps either or both of these extreme views may alternately prevail in future years (it is only forty years since our Spanish adventure) but they each seem too remote for our present decade to bother about.

In between these two extremes I have listed five categories: Enforced isolation; Submissive neutrality; Aggressive neutrality; Singlehanded intervention; Pledged cooperative intervention. The accompanying table (Table 3) shows how all the different schools of thought fall into two different categories of philosophy.

American private opinion will seldom be neutral in any major conflict between other nations, but an official position of taking sides is an entirely different thing and should at all times represent the driving will and desires of the people as a whole. It is the part of each citizen to appraise carefully the character and significance of nations and events and to avoid emotional and conventional judgments before taking sides. Catch phrases such as "democracies against dictatorships" are

TABLE 3

CLASSIFICATION OF ALTERNATIVES

	PRIMARY ENDS	MEANS	
I—Enforced Isolationist	Keep out of war	Maintain indifference to results of foreign wars—abandon foreign vital interests	SELFISH
II—Submissive Neutral	Keep out of war	Maintain impartiality to all belligerents; refuse to fight for foreign vital interests	
III—Aggressive Neutral	Keep out of war	Maintain impartiality to all belligerents	
IV—Singlehanded Interventionist	Assist victims of aggression	Intervene against aggressor	ALTRUISTIC
V—Pledged Cooperative Interventionist	Prevent wars of aggression	Pledge intervention in advance	

misleading. Compare your emotions as you view, on the one hand, a belligerent democracy agressively bulging over its borders, with an absolute dictatorship, in which the citizens are content with their lot within their own boundary. *George S. Montgomery, Jr. International Conciliation. My. '38. p.* 193-208.

AFFIRMATIVE DISCUSSION

NATIONAL DEFENSE PROGRAM [1]

The reasons for maintaining a navy are well known, but I will emphasize a few primary considerations which, together with the facts presented by the political conditions in the world today, justify the provisions of the pending bill to carry out the President's recommendations as contained in his message to Congress of January 28th.

The navy of the United States is maintained for two general reasons. One is the prevention of war. The other is readiness to wage war effectively so that, if forced upon us, war may be brought to a close as quickly as possible with a minimum loss of men and economic resources.

The navy insures our national integrity, supports our national policies, guards the continental United States and our overseas possessions and gives protection to our citizens abroad. The navy can do this effectively only if it is maintained at a strength which will prevent a serious challenge by any nation or nations to any of America's vital national policies, which will insure respect by foreign states and their people for our citizens abroad, and which will make an attack on any part of our territory too costly and too hazardous for any foreign nation or nations to attempt.

The navy does not have in mind any particular possible enemy, but does consider all foreign navies in its study of the sea defense needed by the United States.

[1] From testimony of Admiral W. D. Leahy, U.S.N. before the House Committee on Naval Affairs. *United States. House. Committee on Naval Affairs. Hearings on H. R. 9218.* 1938. p. 1940-2.

The navy has no thought of obtaining assistance from any other nation.

It has no thought of giving assistance in the solution of the problems of any other nation.

It has no foreign commitments.

There are no understandings regarding assistance to be given or received.

There has been no talk of giving or receiving assistance.

The navy expects to solve naval defense problems that may confront the United States in the navy's traditional way without alliances.

It expects to stand on its own feet in providing protection to the United States and it expects to succeed.

When statesmanship has failed to preserve peace, and when the citizens of our country, through their elected representatives in Congress, have decided that war is necessary as a last recort and have declared war, then the responsibility for bringing the war to a close, so far as it can be done by fighting, rests with the armed forces of the nation. It is needless to say that, if war is declared by the Congress, the nation will expect the armed forces to be victorious in order that the ends for which we went to war may be attained, and will expect the armed forces to be in a state of readiness to insure victory.

In defending our territory in war, we cannot assume an attitude of passive defense and simply beat off an attack at one place and later at another. In such a case we would see our coasts blockaded, our outlying possessions seized, our commerce, both coastwise and foreign, driven off the seas, and we would undergo the costly experience of finding the war lasting just as long as the enemy willed it—that is until he had attained every objective and everything he wanted. The only way that war, once begun, can be brought to a successful conclusion is by making the enemy want to stop fighting

—by injuring him so badly that he is ready to quit. Prompt and effective injury to an enemy, at a distance from our shores, is the only correct strategy to be employed.

We have outlying possessions in Alaska, the Hawaiian Islands, Guam, Samoa, Panama, Canal Zone, Puerto Rico, and the Virgin Islands. The Philippine Islands are still United States territory and will remain so until complete independence it attained. All of these outlying possessions are more or less vulnerable and their defense depends upon two factors. One is a local defense by mobile forces and fortification. The other, and the dominant factor, is sea-power. A superior navy can prevent powerful attacks being made on all these outlying possessions that lie closer to our home territory then they do to those of any enemy or enemies. A sufficient navy can keep open the lines of supply to the defenders of such possessions and, if they are secure in their own local defenses against minor attacks, the navy can use them as bases from which to operate against the enemy or enemies. Defense of those possessions (Guam, the Philippines and Alaska) which lie nearer to the home territory of another power or powers than they do to the continental United States, is dependent solely upon sea power and the ability of sea power to support forces in these areas.

A navy cannot be created upon the outbreak of war. If it is inadequate upon the outbreak of war it cannot be increased to adequate strength in a short time. The largest ships require at least three years to build. Smaller vessels, particularly those that can be put in quantity production, can be built in much less time. Trained personnel for combatant ships cannot be quickly created.

Should war be forced upon us, the only combatant ships we shall have to begin that war will be those that are completed when war breaks out and those under construction and nearing completion. The first year or two of a war will have to be fought with the ships and men that we have when the war starts.

The political conditions in the world at this moment, both in Europe and in the Far East, are far more threatening than at any time since 1918 and no improvement is in sight. The major conflict in progress in China has resulted in many grave incidents involving the sovereign rights and interests of the United States and other third powers. The civil war in Spain continues unabated and the threat of a general European conflict is ever present. At our own doors nothing stands in the way of the possible exploitation or seizure of the republics of Central and South America except the Monroe Doctrine, backed by such naval forces as the United States may have and the use of that force if the necessity should arise.

The Treaty of London of 1930 marked the beginning of the breakdown of the principle of limitation of naval armament by agreement, as initiated by the United States and established by the Treaty of Washington of 1922. The next six years, 1930 to 1936, witnessed the violation of treaties and the spoilation of weak nations by those with aggressive policies. It is not surprising that the British Commonwealth of Nations and the Republic of France refused at the London Naval Conference of 1935 to be bound by any quantitative limitation of naval armaments, particularly as Japan refused to participate further in the Conference after her demand for parity was rejected. Italy has, so far, not acceded to the London Treaty of 1936. Great Britain, as soon as she was freed from the limitations of the treaties of 1922 and 1930, immediately embarked on a prodigious rearmament program which includes not only the armed forces but industry as well. Japan, since December 31, 1936, has not been bound by any form of naval limitations and would not even enter into an agreement to exchange information regarding her naval program as is now being exchanged under the London Treaty of 1936 among the United States, the British Commonwealth of Nations, and France. Italy, whose delegates helped to frame the treaty of 1936, is still withholding information regarding her naval construction. Germany and Russia both exchange information with Great Britain, in accordance with bilateral treaties. The recently concluded Italo-German-Japanese Anti-Communist Protocol provides "The competent government agencies of the signatory states shall operate together in reporting to each other the activities of the Comintern, as well as to communicate instructions and defense measures to one another." The complete breakdown of international agreement as to the limitation of armament and the initiation of at least one powerful armament bloc of three nations cannot be questioned.

In the face of international political conditions and our naval needs, the relative strength of the United States Navy, as compared with the naval strength of other naval powers, must be considered. Naval strength does not consist of war vessels alone. It comprises adequate personnel to man the ships; the actual material readiness of the ships; an efficient and adequate aviation component; reserves of men, munitions and supplies; a sufficient number of suitable auxiliary vessels and an efficient merchant marine manned by a loyal personnel; as well as suitable bases located at strategic positions for the repair, docking and maintenance of the vessels and planes. No one factor can be neglected as all are essential to real naval strength.

The strength of the United States navy is determined by law. The Vinson-Trammell Act states that "The composition of the United States navy with respect to the categories of vessels limited by treaties signed at Washington, February 6, 1922, and at London,

April 22, 1930, is hereby established at the limit pre-scribed by those treaties."

The so-called "Treaty navy" established by the treaties of Washington, 1922, and London, 1930, and authorized by the Vinson-Trammell Act was at that time considered to be sufficient in strength to pro-vide adequate defense against attack by any single naval power, and not sufficient in strength to carry an attack to their shores. The navies of Great Britain, the United States, and Japan were by these treaties fixed at a strength ratio of 5-5-3.

These ratios were assumed to provide a correct and an adequate provision for defense against attack by any one of the treaty powers against any other.

It is my opinion that the proportion, 5-5-3, did at that time accomplish this safety precaution against at-tack and that if the treaties had been adhered to there would now be no occasion for increases in the navies.

Subsequent to the failure of the London Conference of 1935 both Great Britain and Japan have commenced enormous increases in their naval power which have completely upset the 5-5-3 ratio; and unless the United States commences without delay a comparable increase in its navy we will in a short time have insufficient security against attack from overseas.

In addition to the rapidly growing naval power of Great Britain and Japan, Italy and Germany are also engaged in an extravagant naval building program, par-ticularly in battleships which are the backbone of naval power, and there is now in existence an Italo-German-Japanese "Anti-Communist Protocol" which must be taken into consideration by America's sea defense.

The moderate increase in naval power for which authorization is provided in the pending bill is necessary to provide defense against attack on our shores by possible enemies in view of foreign naval expansion now well under way.

There is nothing in this program that would permit of aggressive action, of policing the world, or of projecting an attack against the territory of any other naval power.

It would require at least three times the proposed increase to prepare for aggressive action overseas with any reasonable prospect of success.

OUR NAVY TODAY [2]

It was in 1915 that the General Board of the Navy enunciated as a fundamental naval policy that the United States possess a navy equal to that of any other power. This policy met with the approval of the administration, and in order to carry it out a program of naval expansion was inaugurated which was known as the 1916 naval-building program. At the time of our entry into the World war very few of these vessels had passed beyond the blue-print stage. Reasonable statesmen of the World war period believed that had such an American navy been in existence at the time the General Board's policy was formulated, not only would this country have escaped becoming involved but our influence might have brought the conflict to a speedier end and a more enduring peace.

Since that time international agreements among the principal naval powers have accorded world recognition of this country's right to primacy in naval strength. It is significant to note also that thru various changes in political administration our government has adhered steadfastly to the dogma of naval parity with the strongest. This is a right recognized at home and abroad, and a principle that has consistently transcended the debates and issues of partisan politics, tho funds to carry out that principle were not provided. Few persons

[2] By Claude A. Swanson, Secretary of the Navy. *United States. House. Committee on Naval Affairs. Hearings on H. R. 9218.* p. 404-6.

today will question the wisdom of this policy of a navy second to none; nor will they question the two principal reasons for maintaining such a navy: "To support the national policies and commerce" and "to guard the continental and overseas possessions of the United States."

The overwhelming endorsement by Congress in 1933 of the Vinson-Trammell bill, which authorized the upbuilding of our navy to the limitations of international treaties, was in response to the clear mandate of the American people. But our representatives in Congress were not content to stop at mere authorization. Generous appropriations by the Congress and additional funds from public works were earmarked for naval construction by the administration. As a result we have today in various stages of completion 79 ships.

Had the existing treaties remained in effect, by 1942 we would have had our navy up to full treaty strength. Because the powers failed to reach an agreement in London as to quantitative limitations, the navies are no longer stabilized on what many had grown to consider an equitable basis. Now that the rigidity of quantitative restrictions will no longer be observed after this year, it is difficult to forecast what the future holds for naval building. We of the navy do not expect and would deplore any navy building race. The policy of the Navy Department is not to build an excessive number of warships over a short period of time. Our industrial plants are capable of carrying only so much building load efficiently and economically. The requirements of research and experimentation also dictate a slow, progressive building program over a number of years. Such a program is far superior to the spasmodic policy that has characterized so much of our building in the past. Periodic replacements of obsolescent vessels and modest additions to our fleet need give rise to no concern by others; whereas alternate periods of neglect succeeded by feverish expansion may result in misunderstanding and misinterpretation by other nations.

The present naval building program for combatant vessels is considered by the Navy Department as satisfactory under existing conditions. It should result in giving to us a combatant fleet adequate in numbers and efficient as individual units.

Sea power comprehends more than a navy of combatant ships and planes. Naval bases and a merchant marine are the two other elements that together with the fighting navy constitute sea power in its broadest term. The number of naval bases are more or less fixed. They are dependent upon geographic considerations and new bases are difficult to acquire. A merchant marine is essential to the prosperity of any modern industrial state at all times and is a potential source of auxiliary vessels and personnel in wartime. This last consideration is of great importance. The larger the merchant marine in peace, the more auxiliaries it can provide for the navy in wartime.

The combatant fleet, however, requires naval auxiliaries that must operate and train with the fleet during peace time as well as in war. The Vinson-Trammell bill authorizes the construction and replacement within treaty limitations of all combatant types. A bill now before Congress would provide a greater number of suitable auxiliaries to support this combat craft. The mission of these auxiliaries will be to make effective, thru the function of service and supply, the fighting vessels of our fleet. That fleet in fulfilling its mission of naval protection to the homeland in time of war must take up its station far from normal bases of supply and repair. This fact is often lost sight of by earnest advocates of national defense. To be effective the combatant vessels of our navy must be so mobile and self-sufficient that they can be projected a thousand miles or more from our coast and be maintained on their far-distant stations. This, in effect, will create a new elastic frontier of steel. Behind this frontier will lie an oceanic hinterland of millions of square miles. Over this buffer state an enemy must launch an air attack before it reaches the valuable and vulnerable cities of our coast line. The dimensions of this neutral region are contingent not alone upon the number of our fighting ships. To maintain our combatant vessels upon this far-flung frontier, to preserve its elasticity by insuring the mobility of the individual ships and units, these vessels must be sustained from the homeland by a constantly cruising fleet of auxiliaries.

It is true that in wartime many of these auxiliaries can be improvised from our merchant marine, provided we keep intact that great adjunct of national prosperity. It would be not only impracticable but a needless waste to provide our navy in peacetime with all of the auxiliaries it would need in any major war operation that sought to destroy or defeat any enemy fleet before it came within striking distance of our shores. The merchant marine will continue to be the main reservoir of our auxiliaries. But there are a certain number of highly specialized types of auxiliaries that cannot be improvised from the merchant craft overnight, that are needed with the fleet in its normal peacetime cruising and that, above all else, must be trained with the fleet.

NAVAL EXPANSION PROGRAM [3]

As I understand the situation, at all the naval armament conferences we have been at a disadvantage in bringing about a real limitation of naval armament, because, aside from the Washington agreement, we were never in the position to make sacrifice of naval vessels. We were always inferior and below the ratio of 5-5-3.

[3] From speech by David I. Walsh, Senator from Massachusetts. *Congressional Record.* 83:7300-17. April 19, 1938.

When we pleaded for lowering the number and tonnage of naval craft, we were confronted with the argument, by both Great Britain and Japan, that we were asking those countries to scrap and not doing any scrapping ourselves.

We could not scrap, because we were below the 5-5-3 ratio. It is reported by those who represented us at the conferences that the fact which I have stated was a decided disadvantage. The statesmen of the other countries were embarrassed at the prospect of returning to their people and stating that they had sunk millions of dollars worth of naval craft, and that the United States, the richest country of all, had made no sacrifices.

Testimony was given before our committee quoting Lloyd George as saying that if, upon the outbreak of the World war in 1914, the United States had proceeded to build up a strong and powerful navy, we never would have been in the World war. That is what Lloyd George said; and why? Because Germany and Great Britain, both of which imposed upon our rights on the sea, would have been afraid to do so, and neither Germany nor Great Britain would have wanted us to be on the opposite side from them in the war.

I am very much impressed with that statement— that had we, at the outbreak of the World war, built up the powerful navy which we had at the end of the war, we would have avoided a tremendous expenditure, we would have saved the lives of many, many human beings that were lost in the war, and in all probability we would have entirely escaped the war.

* * *

I do not see how we can escape the responsibility of building up a navy that will be adequate and will have some chance in conflict to protect us against an enemy.

I cannot conceive of anything worse than having an impotent navy, ships going up and down the coast afraid of an enemy, a navy which will not come out and meet the enemy before they begin to bombard our cities, a navy that is conscious of its weaknesses, which realizes that the other navy has six more powerful battleships, has double the number of submarines and cruisers, has triple the number of airplanes. What would be a wise and sensible policy for the head of the navy except to hug the shore, as poor Germany had to do during the World war, afraid to go out, knowing that the ships would be lost, as they were finally destroyed?

WAR CLOUDS OVER AMERICA [4]

Many of our good citizens deplore American preparation for war. They hold that if, as we profess, we are a peace loving people, it is inconsistent to build up a fighting navy and a great air fleet; that if other nations are so foolish as to prepare for war and therefore in a sense invite it, that is exclusively their affair and none of our business and that we should ignore the whole of the mad scramble for military superiority and go quietly along with our peaceful pursuits as though nothing unusual was occurring. As a matter of course we all sympathize with a peaceful philosophy and probably none more so than those who are responsible for the welfare of the nation. The difference of opinion is wholly upon the point of what course is best calculated to keep us out of war.

It is with nations very much as it is with individuals. There are situations in which the most law abiding, peace respecting, cultured man in the world, a man who never engaged in argument, who never had had a quarrel in his life, who always graciously ignored an insult

[4] From article by L. W. Rogers. *Ancient Wisdom.* 4:5. March 1938.

from weaker and more ignorant people, would be compelled to use force. If he saw a brutal man furiously beating a child and should find that his energetic protests were unavailing he would use physical force in defense of the child. If he saw a murder being committed he would rush instantly to the defense of the victim and disarm the murderer, if that were possible, or knock him senseless if that were necessary. In defense of his wife or children he would, if absolutely necessary, kill a murderous assailant when the only question at issue was whose life must be lost. Situations sometimes arise in which killing, horrible as it is, cannot be avoided.

A good way in which to see more clearly the principles involved in the present state of affairs among the nations is to step down the problem to smaller and less complex terms. Let us suppose then that nations are simply individual people and that we are merely dealing with Mr. Mussolini and his family, Mr. Franco and his wife and children, Mr. John Bull and his progeny, Mr. Hitler and his uncles and his cousins, Mr. Jappo and his lusty sons, Mr. Stalin and his wife and babies and Uncle Samuel and his happy family. All goes well in this peaceful community for many years and everybody is on friendly terms with everybody else. None of these neighbors have more firearms than is customary for protection against robbers and other violators of the rules of civil life. It is not only agreed amongst them that all disputes that may arise shall be settled by arbitration with never a resort to force but also that there shall be no offenses against more distant neighbors, such as there had been in the far past when less civilized customs were general. But one day Mr. Mussolini, when strolling far from home, observed that the farm of Mr. Ethiope was not only large and productive but also grew the particular crops that the Mussolini family urgently needed. Being a far more powerful person than the proprietor he thereupon chased the owner off and took possession. The neighbors in our little community were indignant. They called a meeting and adopted strong resolutions of protest and threatened to stop the exchange of products with the Mussolini family unless the wrong was set right. But when time passed and nothing dreadful happened to the Mussolinis Mr. Jappo decided to try his luck at the same trick. After spending much time in accumulating arms and ammunition that gave him and his sons enormously greater power than the more numerous family of his neighbor, he fought his way into their home and took possession, after killing several members of the assaulted family. Again the community neighbors vehemently protested. The only effect was that Mr. Mussolini and Mr. Hitler congratulated Mr. Jappo for his good taste in selecting an easy victim to despoil and all three began arming themselves more perfectly.

Now what, under the circumstances, should the peace loving neighbors of our little community do? They are not left to guess about any point in the problem. They know that two well armed neighbors have renounced their solemnly signed agreement not to resort to armed force and have persisted in plundering peaceful neighbors regardless of the protests and threats of the whole community. They know that an alliance has been formed to include a third like-minded neighbor to assist them in any future difficulties that may arise. They know that these people are utterly unscrupulous once they start upon a plundering carouse; that they will not hesitate at murder; that their philosophy is that "to the victor belong the spoils"; that they will take by armed force whatever they can and keep it for their own; and that they will no more hesitate to murder and rob their neighbors in the community than those outside it. What, then, should the peace loving neighbors do, arm themselves to the point of safety or pass a resolution informing the lawless ones that if they treat them as they did the despoiled neighbors they, the peace lovers, will surely slap such bandits upon the wrist? There are times when peace talk is very valuable. There are conditions and another time when it is simply silly, and we seem to have reached it.

Naturally we all regret keenly even the shadow of the war cloud over the United States. But regrets do not soften the hearts of those who cheerfully set about the job of bombing thousands of women and children in order to crush the national spirit and render the government subservient to the will of the invaders. War lords understand but one argument—that which is emphasized with a physical force equal to or greater than their own.

We may fortunately never need the greater navy which it is proposed to build just as you may not need the umbrella you carry on a threatening day; but it would be foolish not to take it. The present situation recalls the story of the eastern tourist in Texas a half century ago. "Why," he said to a Texan who had a pistol in his belt, "do people go armed here? It seems to be a very peaceful country." To which the old Texan replied, "Well, young feller, you might live around here a long time and not need a gun but if you ever did need it you'd want it bad!" And so it may be with the new navy. We may regret the necessity for building it but if a sudden shift of international events developed a desperate need for it when we had none our regret that we were unprepared to meet an emergency might be a thousand times keener.

PEACE-AT-ALL-COSTISM [5]

There are in general two kinds of isolationists. There are the peace-at-all-costers, gentle, well-meaning

[5] From article by Walter Shaw. *Dynamic America.* 6:11-14. June, 1938.

people who would rather let Dictator Foolem come to Washington than resist him. They agonize over the horrors of war and conflict, forgetting the horrors of tyranny and despotism which are permanent, not temporary as war is. They seem to be possessed by some naive fancy that by sufficiently turning the other cheek, by a policy of appeasement, the dictators may be dissuaded from their evil purposes, and the world will be transformed into sweetness and light. I don't know what to say to these sweet ladies and gentlemen, except that life doesn't work that way. Nor can we appeal to the aggressor peoples over the heads of their rulers, because all their avenues of information are muzzled and controlled. Naturally, if we are willing to make concessions indefinitely until we have nothing left, even to the extent of handing over our own government, we can have a certain peace.

But the worst horrors of war are not in death and suffering. These are a part also of peace—perhaps part of the lot of man. The worst horrors lie in the spiritual death, fear, suspicion, the hatred of man for man; not in any atrocity, but in the minds made capable of perpetrating atrocity, in the prostitution of all moral standards, in the destruction of all dissenting opinion, all impartial justice, all individual freedom.

Just these same horrors happen under despotism. A peace perpetuating the very things that make war repugnant is not an aspiration worth striving for. It differs from war only in having a less rapid velocity of bloodshed, and unlike war there is no armistice after which reconstruction can begin.

I believe there are things worth fighting for, namely, freedom, brotherhood, justice! I believe there are things worse than war, namely despotism, oppression and the decay and degeneration that would follow universal tyranny. I don't believe in peace at all costs. I believe in peace if we have to fight for it, or even if we have to die for it.

The second type of isolationist believes in "minding our own business," staying within our own borders, fighting if we have to, but not until our country is attacked. The issue then becomes: can we best avoid trouble by planning against it or waiting until it is right on top of us? In short, shall we try to prevent trouble or simply try to avoid it?

If 1914 was a selfish scramble for spoils from which we might better have remained aloof, there is no question today who the aggressors are. China did not invade Japan. Ethiopia did not attack Italy. In fact the pretext for Italian invasion was a troop skirmish a hundred miles within the Ethiopian border.

Morally-minded people are constantly reminding us that England and France as well as ourselves are by no means without blemish when it comes to imperialism and conquest. We are hypocritical they assert or at least inconsistent if we now begin censuring others for doing the same thing.

The democracies, of course, are far from perfect, but the gulf that separates them from the Fascists is tremendous. Never have they descended to the flagrant breaking of pledges, the wholesale and ruthless slaughter that marked the Japanese invasion of China or the Italian invasion of Ethiopia. The worst atrocity-lies of the World war, the callous destruction of hospitals, the massacre and torture of prisoners, the terrorizing of non-combatants and helpless minorities, are today not only admitted as good tactical strategy, but even boasted of as somehow exemplifying the glory and might of the conquerors.

If democracies pursue evil policies, at least there is freedom at home to protest against them. Here at least there is an unfettered press to print the real facts, and an independent public opinion that already has exerted great pressure for change. Today England is giving increasing freedom to India. France is giving autonomy to Syria. America has withdrawn from Haiti and Nicaragua and is giving self-government to the Philippines.

We cannot undo the past, but we can and must concern ourselves vitally with the future. Even if the democracies were once equally guilty, the fact that past criminals have "gotten away with it" would be a poor argument for allowing things to keep on that way forever.

The fact is simply that the thing has to stop some time. We may not be particularly concerned with what happens in Czechoslovakia, or Spain, as a nation; but we are vitally concerned with living in the kind of world where we ourselves can enjoy the security of international law and order. If a few despots ruling over slave-states can keep on swallowing up territory after territory, it's a cinch that sooner or later we ourselves will be on the *carte du jour*.

You can hear their dreams of world domination taught in their school rooms. Impossible, you say, that America could ever be threatened. Why more impossible than Japanese guns along the Whangpoo? Why more impossible than Italian planes over Madrid? If the Dictators send their troops into barren Ethiopia, into the wastes of Manchukuo, why should the center of the world's civilization and industry remain immune? Indeed, as long as the traditions of liberty and free government survive in the new world, how could any despotism feel secure in the old? Why do the Nazis finance storm troops in South America? Why does Japan build an ever bigger navy if her only opponents are China and Russia who have no fleet? Not now, perhaps, not in our lifetime. But we would hardly be worthy of our heritage if we closed our eyes to save our own skins, only to have the axe fall on the necks of our children. Three thousand miles of water are not as wide as they used to be, and they're getting narrower every day.

What will stop them? Will they be stopped by pledges not to attack? Whose pledges? Pledges of the man who swore to uphold the German Republic; who promised Austria independence? Pledges of the man bound by the League Covenant to respect Ethiopia's sovereignty? Pledges of the nation bound by the Nine Power Pact against Chinese aggression? Or of the two Dictators whose nations remain as members of the Spanish Non-Intervention Committee, even while boasting in the home newspapers of their military conquests? The strategists of the new *Machtpolitik* are on a plane of morality above that of ordinary men. They do not need to be bound by promises. And pledges instead of being binding agreements are conceived as strategic weapons to befuddle your opponents, like the boxer who feints for the belly and strikes at the jaw.

Will they be stopped by concessions, raw materials, and colonies for expansion? Italy won her Ethiopia, but instead of settling it and exploiting its wealth she moves against Spain. Japan won her Manchukuo, Hopei, Jehol, doubling her territory. But instead of developing its new wealth, she moves against central China. These nations do not want *equality* — they want *dominance!* Concessions merely whet their appetite and shift the balance of power in their favor. The ancient Saxon kings paid money to the Danes not to invade England. The Danes kept taking the money, and when the kings went broke they conquered England anyway.

Will they be stopped by ethical scruples? Read the answer in the bombed Spanish hospitals, in the ashes of Guarnica and Adowa, in the ruins of Barcelona and Shanghai.

Will they be stopped by internal collapse? What internal revolt would have a chance in the face of continued foreign successes?

Will they be stopped by fighting each other? Why should they as long as they can find softer pickings in the rich pacifistic democracies?

Will they be stopped by a combination of powers arrayed against them? Perhaps, but only by joint collective action. No single nation can do it. And we can hardly advocate for others a course of action we are unwilling to undertake ourselves.

The march of the despots will be stopped only when circumstances make it prudent for them to alter their tactics, not by concessions or beautiful phrases, but by the threat of superior force. The psychology of despotism is that of a typical bully, shouting the loudest when his opponent is running away. When British ships entered the Mediterranean the "pirate" submarine disappeared. In 1934 when Italian troops concentrated on the Austrian frontier Hitler backtracked rapidly. They fear general war, dread it more than anything in the world, knowing that defeat would mean their destruction. Yet by an incredible supineness or stupidity they are permitted to strengthen themselves on weak isolated nations, growing stronger and more menacing at every swallow.

What does collective security mean? It means that as a great power America shall take the responsibility of a great power, not to join any existing alliance, but to rally like minded nations around us. This does not mean that America should police the world. That is obviously impossible. It does mean that we should keep lines of defense outside our own borders, and not wait until the thing is right on top of us.

It doesn't mean that we're *against* anybody, or that we will go to war to undo the past, to drive Hitler out of Austria or Mussolini out of Ethiopia. It does mean, however, that we will draw the line as far as the future is concerned.

A reasonable program of collective security should distinguish between economic and military action. Economically, we could cooperate thruout the world by sanctions against the aggressor, using our resources to strengthen the victimized nations.

Militarily we would act only when the thing got uncomfortably near to us, namely in the event of an attack on the South American republics, or if Britain and France in a war *against* aggression were in danger of defeat.

NAVAL EXPANSION PROGRAM [6]

Nations have but one means of protecting their rights across the sea and that means is their navy. Unfortunately, that all-vital function of our own navy is often lost sight of, and instead of considering the navy as the defense for our vital rights across the sea we find it sometimes thought of as only a coast defense, as a defense for our homeland. Of course, a navy sufficient to protect our rights across the sea will automatically insure safety to our coasts. But it does not follow that a meager navy such as would be sufficient for our coastal protection would be any protection at all across the sea.

If we are to keep what we have, we must have a navy strong enough to prevent interference by force with our rights across the sea. Not to have such a navy is to invite the denial of those rights and to increase the probability of a war to regain them. But having it, and with other nations knowing its power, interference with our rights would become most unlikely and, therefore, the most probable cause of war for us would be eliminated.

[6] From testimony of Rear Admiral Harris Laning before the Senate Committee on Naval Affairs. *United States. Senate. Committee on Naval Affairs. Hearings on H.R. 9218. 1938. p. 411-13.*

Under such circumstances, can we doubt what we should want? It is a navy that not only will insure us our rights across the sea and the continued well-being and prosperity of our people thru trade, but at the same time will insure us against actions that start war and, therefore, will insure us against war itself.

Vital as a sufficient navy is to us in insuring peace and prosperity to our people, such a navy will be of even greater benefit to us should war come.

The remarkable effect of naval power in war is little understood. We are prone to think of war in terms of military forces and to measure its awful costs in lives and blood of armies. However, in a war against a maritime nation, such as any great war for us will be, a sufficient navy can do more to reduce the horrible costs than can any other agency. As examples of that we have only to understand the use of naval power even in such wars as our own Civil war or in the World war. Altho in both wars long land fronts were covered and enormous armies used, nevertheless it was the almost bloodless naval blockade that in each denied to enemy armies essential fighting material, that kept from enemy peoples what they required for existence, and that ultimately so crushed the will of those people to fight that their governments sought peace at any price. What might have been the cost of either war in blood and treasure or even what might have been the ultimate result had there been insufficient naval power on our side, no one knows. But it is certain that thru the effective use of superior naval power both wars were greatly shortened, the costs to us in money and blood were tremendously reduced, and the ultimate welfare of our people was assured. So always the effect of a proper navy on a war.

Desiring peace, wishing to keep what we have without war, and above all, wanting to reduce the bloodiness of war, what better can we do than provide ourselves with the navy that will insure those things to us? What then should our navy be to insure them?

Such a navy was authorized for us in the Washington Treaty. By that treaty, naval strengths, tho limited, were so balanced that no one signatory power had sufficient strength to interfere with the rights of another signatory power without danger of being defeated in war. With the authorized balances established by that treaty lived up to, war between any of the great powers signing it became unlikely. But today that treaty is no longer in effect. Nations are no longer limited in what they can build, and the greatest step toward peace we ever made—the balancing of naval power—no longer exists.

However, altho there is no established balance in naval power which, if lived up to, will practically insure peace, we can still insure peace to the United States if we maintain for ourselves the relative naval power established for us by the Washington Treaty. Altho nations are no longer limited in what they can build, we ourselves can still have all the good of the Washington Treaty, except as regards money cost, if we maintain the ratio of naval strength established for us by that treaty. If in each class of ships we maintain not less than a 5-to-5 ratio with Great Britain and a 5-to-3 ration with Japan, we will make war unlikely for us, will insure the well-being and prosperity of our people, will shorten any war we may be forced into, and will tremendously reduce the war's cost to us in treasure and blood.

ISOLATION, COOPERATION AND PEACE [7]

Roughly estimated, there are three lines of thought, as follows: those who regard both war and our entrance into it as inevitable; those who think that nothing can stop a general war, but that the United States can remain

[7] From article by *Elizabeth M. Lynsky. Commonweal. My.* 20, '38. *p.* 94.

out of it, or on the sidelines; those who think that war need not come at all. In the first group are probably the majority of extremists of both left and right economic views. Probably the greater part of Americans are in class two, advocates of one or another form of isolation or neutrality. In the first and third groups one finds all those who would support any form of cooperative action, for varied and often for opposite reasons.

Take the case of the advocates of isolation, who argue that America can and must stay out of a general war, either by stopping trade with foreign nations altogether, or by declaring our neutrality in any foreign war. Such a person either believes that this nation is or can be separated from all foreign interests of any sort, or he believes that sanity has fled from foreign shores to abide here as a last resting-place. The isolationist whose views arise from nationalism does one of two things: he argues for a return to the ideas of neutrality that preceded the Great war (the freedom of the seas, and the attempt to confine war geographically to the belligerents, within legal boundaries of military necessity, sovereign responsibility, and humanity); or he refuses to defend American foreign trade and investments, argues for national self-sufficiency and national economic planning, jeers at "humanizing" warfare, and speaks feelingly of "buying American" and "minding our own business." On the other hand, the isolationist whose convictions spring from humanitarian idealism or religious pacifism sees in the nation which resorts to modern war a society less than human, from which he recoils. Devoted to humane ideas, cultural and personal values, and oftentimes to ideals of democratic government, he wishes to preserve "civilization" in one corner of a crazy world. He would have the United States withdraw as it were within its citadel of plenty and beauty, and close the gates upon the clamor of the hungry in outer darkness.

In either case portrayed above, if the isolationist is consistent, he must favor a large navy or a large army, or both. If he wishes to maintain old-fashioned neutrality, he must realize that the freedom of the seas can be maintained by neutrals only by their willingness to enforce the principle. Sometimes, as in the last war, the attempt to keep the seas free for neutral shipping may draw neutrals into the war, whereupon they cease to be neutral and often lose interest in the freedom of the seas. If the isolationist prefers to have his nation withdraw entirely from foreign trade in time of war, he must permit his government to defend this decision against those fighting nations whose chance to win the war may be harmed by the decision, as also against discontent from within the isolated state. Seldom will the isolationist admit this necessity for armaments. He confuses neutrality and isolation with peace and tranquility. He admits that within the state the conflicting interests of citizens require the institution of courts and police force to gain the public ends for which the state exists—peace and order, justice and freedom for the individual. He does not see, or will not admit, that human migration, trade and investment beyond national borders gain other human ends of an economic character—a higher standard of living, and a wider cultural knowledge, and that these ends, too, require courts and a police force to prevent their conflict from becoming chaos. He may agree that in times past, war has served as a means of maintaining treaties and providing an order in which men might migrate and trade; but he can no longer tolerate war, even to preserve human relations. The nationalist or humanitarian who repudiates war and demands isolation repudiates international exchange of goods and ideas, often without realizing that he must plan to enlarge national forces if he is to reorganize the economic life of his country. If, instead, he repudiates war and demands neutrality, he insists upon retaining the human values of international interdependence, but fails to perceive that he still requires force to defend neutrality against belligerents.

BRIEF EXCERPTS

If we rest on our old foreign policy of protecting our interests wherever they may be it stands to reason that the more warships we have the less chance there will be of our having to use them. The converse it true also. The smaller our naval strength, the greater the chance of receiving insults from Japan which will arouse sentiment in this country to war pitch. *Edwin L. James. New York Times. Ja.* 30, '38. *Sec.* 4. *p.* 8.

Had the United States prior to the assassination at Sarajevo possessed an armed force commensurate with the wealth, the resources and the population of the nation, we might have been able to hold aloof from what so quickly followed. Had we been sufficiently powerful, we might indeed have prevented the World war from taking place. *Col. Edward M. House. New York Times. Mr.* 24, '37. *p.* 15.

The chairman (Round Table on Methods and Procedure for Peace) suggested that disarmament had failed as a substitute for war; the large amount of attention given it had led to little which was effective. Disarmament alone will not and cannot act as a substitute for war. It will save money and build up confidence and security, but it must be regarded as only a part of the general peace program. *Institute of World Affairs. Proceedings.* 1936. *p.* 179.

It is the conviction of many, including Mr. Roosevelt, that our present and future building program are perfectly in accord with our aims toward the limitation of armaments. Certainly the success of the Washington Conference was largely due to our vast, potential strength at that time. Because of our geographical position, we

must take the lead in future disarmament discussion—
when any lead is taken. And it will be far more effective, if, instead of saying, "Why don't you scrap your
ships down to our level?" we are able to say, "Let us
put aside these arms together." *John C. Winslow. Current History. My. '38. p. 20.*

Arms have restored English prestige and there is no
doubt that British rearmament plans are the outstanding
peace factor on the Continent today. What a peace machinery at conference tables could not accomplish—a war
machinery did.

Rearmament serves Britain a twofold purpose: she
can now show her might and in so doing prevent attack;
and if she has to fight she will be ready for it. Its repercussions have been felt in Berlin, Rome, and Tokyo.
While the White Paper did not mention any possible
enemy, it contained a statement that no foreign dictator
or military chief could have overlooked, that "at present
there is no justification for any reduction or slowing
down of the program." *Curt L. Heymann. Current History. Ag. '37. p. 45.*

For the assumption so frequently made that any nation
possessed of a large navy will inevitably succumb to the
temptation to use it aggressively, there seems small
warrant in history, certainly in American history. The
United States' periods of jingoism have not coincided
with its period of greatest naval strength. During the
expansionist forties and fifties of the last century, when
"manifest destiny" was a popular slogan, the United
States had a weak fleet and a large commerce exposed
to ruin in the event of war. During the years 1915 to
1921, the country's most rapid period of naval construction, its thinking was essentially defensive. *James Phinney Baxter. Christian Science Monitor Weekly Magazine Section. Mr. 9, '38. p. 2.*

The only justification of British rearmament is that it will serve to buttress the rule of law against force, that it will contribute to the creation of a system of collective security under the League of Nations which will deter other heavily armed powers from aggression against Britain and other law-abiding and peace-loving members of the League, and that in the meantime a constructive policy of economic and military disarmament will be resolutely and consistently pursued. It must be made abundantly clear to the world that we are willing to stop our rearmament program the moment other nations are willing to join us in general disarmament. *Archibald Sinclair. Contemporary Review. Ap. '37. p.* 391-2.

An armed dictatorship makes it necessary for other countries either, tacitly, to accept its will in advance or to make themselves sufficiently strong to oppose it. No dictator will fight if he is not supremely confident that he will win—except as a measure of desperation, when his own downfall is imminent. That being so, the chief hope of escape from a European war lies in the ability of the democratic power to satisfy the first requisite of democracy, which is the power to defend itself and thus perpetuate its own existence. This is no threat to the peoples living under dictatorships: it is merely a means to prevent the extension of the evils from which they themselves suffer. *Prof. J. H. Jones. Accountant (Lond.) N. 27, '37. p.* 720.

The futility of diplomacy when divorced from adequate force, the danger of being drawn into war from weakness, and the peaceful security that is inherent in military-naval strength, are principles that have many illustrations in American history. From this point of view the following episodes, besides the foregoing, are well worthy of critical examination: the quasi-naval War with France (1798-1801), our wars with the Mediterranean

Barbary Powers, the War of 1812, the War with Mexico, the occupation of Mexico by the French during our Civil war and their subsequent evacuation, the crisis with Japan during the administration of President Theodore Roosevelt, and our entry into the World war. *Capt. Dudley W. Knox. Atlantic Monthly. Ap. '38. p. 497.*

The French, who contended that security must precede disarmament, were right in their thesis if not in their methods. Only the assurance of joint action by the strongest powers against any aggressor could—if anything could—have induced reduction of armaments. Only a real prospect of peaceful revision of treaties and frontiers could—if anything could—have led the dissatisfied nations to become reconciled to the collective system.

But it has not yet been possible to attain either such a guaranteed peace or such a flexible and conciliatory peace, and so both the collective system and the hope of disarmament have failed thus far. *Harold Callender. New York Times Magazine. S. 8, '35. p. 7.*

The bill is not a militaristic movement but distinctly a peace measure. It serves notice on every citizen in the land that the full power of the government will be used to prevent profiteering and that no citizen can expect to profit from any war in which we might be engaged. In this way the bill kills any incentive that anyone might have to do anything that might encourage, provoke or lead to war. We foresee only peace for our country and all that we ask is that our country shall live in peace, in friendship and in cooperation with all the other nations, but the passage of the bill would bring to the attention of other nations the fact that if we were again forced into war our whole economic, industrial and financial life would be effectively and efficiently mobilized for the protection of our country. We ask passage of this bill as one more important step to the great goal of peace. *Report of House Committee on Military Affairs on H.R. 6704. Congressional Digest. Mr. '38. p. 83.*

If Britain is to make a substantial contribution toward the establishment of what is our strongest interest [peace] we must be strongly armed.

I cannot see any object in trying to make a difference between armaments required for defense and armaments required for the purpose of fulfilling international obligations.

There is no question of our using our armaments for purposes of aggression or for purposes inconsistent with the covenant [of the League].

If ever the time comes when the world establishes an international police force which would inspire us all with full confidence in its capacity to keep peace, then there would be no need for us to trouble our heads about our own defense. *British Prime Minister Neville Chamberlain. New York Times. Mr. 25, '38. p. 11.*

Actually, and whether the more idealistic citizens like it or not, the risk of war is always inversely proportional to the risk of making it. Where the risk of making war is too great to be faced the risk of war is too small to be measured. The realistic inquiry at any given moment is the inquiry as to degree of the war-maker's risk.

One element in the computation of that risk is armaments. There are obviously others. There are geographic considerations. There are considerations of money and food and raw materials and manpower. But armaments are nevertheless of the first importance and for this reason: the potential aggressor powers are almost always aggressive because of their dissatisfaction with the economic status quo. They are therefore by definition the powers with inferior economic resources. It

follows that their reliance will be chiefly upon military superiority and that the margin of their military superiority over the peace-loving powers may be the margin between their choice of war and their choice of peace.
Background of War. Fortune. Jl. '37. p. 69.

The keynote of America's program of national defense has been struck by Colonel House, confidant of President Wilson, who knew more about the underlying causes of the World war than any other American. He says:

Paradoxical as it may seem, the only way we can bring the world to its senses and protect our own integrity is to build an adequate army and navy ourselves. We are in a position to build up a war force that could be the most potent instrument for peace in all the world.

But we will not be easily led into war, if on the one hand we build up a powerful peace sentiment, while on the other we make ourselves so strong that our rights will be universally respected. The movements for peace and for preparedness must go together.

Lieut. Col. Adam E. Potts. Peace or War; a Conference. Univ. of Minnesota Press. Minneapolis. Je. '37. p. 178.

I do not believe that a modern city can exist without a police force to repress crime or without courts to enforce contracts. No more do I believe that the modern world can exist without agencies of order and justice. We have tried and the results are before us. Gangster nations have broken loose and declared their intention to seize what they want.

For America to imagine that it can stand aloof in this crisis is as if Brooklyn should retire behind the East River and refuse to concern itself with anarchy in New York. To exactly the extent that Brooklyn kept order and prosperity, it would become the object of the desires of the New York gangsters, and would have to arm to protect itself.

If democracy is to survive this crisis, the democratic nations must organize at once and declare their intention to enforce law and order thruout civilization. Gangster nations planning raids must know not merely that they will be boycotted completely, but that if this does not suffice, an international army and navy will overthrow their dictators, hold a plebiscite, and establish a new government by popular consent. *Upton Sinclair. Nation. Ap.* 2, '38. *p.* 377.

In the last resort I see no escape from armed resistance to aggression. I do not believe that at this stage we are justified in expanding our armaments, either by land or by sea. Our preparedness for the present should consist in the clarification of our objectives as a democracy. If we stress military preparedness now we risk militarism; if we enact dictatorial mobilization laws we shall have fascism at the outbreak of any war, and the battle will be lost before it begins. *R. L. Duffus. Nation. Ap.* 2, '38. *p.* 378.

While South and Central American people have always resented anything that looked like protection on the part of the United States, many of them now hold, much against their will, that the United States navy is all that stands between them and European and Asiatic invasion. They have recently been thoroly disillusioned as to the value of treaties as they watched members of the League of Nations and signatories to the Briand-Kellogg antiwar pact invading territory of others.

Therefore, they have begun to look toward the United States for protection against any attempt to repeat similar invasions on the Western Hemisphere, which is rich in raw materials but is poor in population and military strength. Certain South American foreign offices recently have been exchanging views on a project for a vast inter-American military and naval alliance by which all

South and Central American armies and navies would cooperate with United States forces in repelling any attempted invasion of any American country. *John W. White. New York Times. F.* 20, '38. *p.* 5.

History of the world and our own past experience demonstrate that proper military preparedness subjects a nation to less likelihood of having its rights violated and less likelihood of hostile attack. Hence it is our duty not only to ourselves but also to the cause of civilization to maintain an adequate army and navy. After all, the first obligation of a nation is self-preservation and that with honor.

We believe that the present international armament race should be curtailed and for several years have made strenuous but unsuccessful efforts to that end. While other nations are arming, however, we certainly cannot adopt unilateral disarmament for ourselves alone—a method we tried so disastrously for the twelve years between 1922 and 1933, in assuming "leadership" among the nations of the world almost to the point of our undoing. The resulting reputation of weakness which we earned by this criminally foolish gesture set us back as a world power by almost a generation. Our security depends solely upon ourselves and the necessary force we can muster in times of emergency to protect our country and our democratic ideals. Nor can we do this sucessfully without an adequate and efficient army and navy in proportion to the size, importance and wealth of our country, and its prestige among the nations of the world. *Rear Admiral C. H. Woodward. Vital Speeches. Ap.* 1, '38. *p.* 372-3, 374-5.

A study of the aerial defense of our eastern frontier indicates that if certain air bases were occupied by an enemy force, possessing air equipment as outlined, that our entire industrial area with thousands of profitable targets, as well as the Panama Canal so essential to the maneuvering of our fleet, would be vulnerable to aerial attack.

The task of the aerial defense of all these vital targets by the use of pursuit aviation and anti-aircraft artillery would be practically insurmountable.

The determination of the requisite strength of our air force must be based upon considerations of international relations. If and when the great European conflict occurs, the only way in which the neutral nations in the world can keep out of that conflict is to have such a strong national defense that none of the belligerents involved dare violate their neutrality. Had we had, in 1917, an effective air force, a powerful navy and army comparable to even that of Italy, Germany would not have dared to continue her submarine warfare and thereby force us into the fight on the side of her enemies. Who will say that under the condition of strained international relations existing today, the cost of an adequate air force is too great to pay to keep us out of war? *Major-General O. Westover. Vital Speeches. Ja. 1, '37. p. 182, 184.*

If our navy is weak, we must, in order to provide ourselves with an adequate defense, rely on some friendly ally. If, however, we are to rely only on ourselves, we must have a navy completely adequate for defensive purposes.

Every one will agree that today the world is in a turmoil. Dictatorships are everywhere increasing their armed forces and their strength.

Japan and her dependencies have 97,000,000 people today, armed, militarized and mobilized. Germany has 75,000,000 people completely militarized and ready to go to war. Italy and her dependencies have 58,000,000 people armed and arming, and from the news this morning apparently Spain may soon fall into her lap. Russia has the largest army ever known.

Democracies today are on trial. If they are going to survive they have got to be ready to defend themselves. This applies more to the United States than to any other democracy.

We as a nation believe in peace; we do not want war. We have too much at stake to procrastinate. We have too much at stake to quibble over the adequacy of our defensive naval strength. *Representative Robert L. Bacon. New York Times. Mr.* 17, '38. *p.* 8.

We Americans cannot understand the contemporary world unless we take cognizance of the philosophical outlook of other great peoples and shape our national policies in the knowledge that their ways are not necessarily our ways.

The patriotic Japanese, for example, cannot comprehend the American exaltation of peace. He looks upon our pacifism as a sign of national decay—when he believes it to be genuine. Otherwise, he thinks it is a hypocritical pretense calculated to fool the unwary. Certain Japanese diplomats are not averse to cultivating American pacifist sentiment for the purpose of obtaining political concessions in the way of arms limitation and similar agreements, but they do not respect the mental attitude which inspires pacifism. They would not tolerate such an attitude in Japan. Nor would Soviet Russia, which long ago jailed Tolstoyans when they raised their heads, and is today one of the foremost military powers.

As one nurtured in the principles of the oldest Christian pacifist sect and acquainted at first hand with the realities of war, I certainly have no desire to see the martial virtues exalted in this country. But I see only harm arising out of our lack of comprehension of the true nature of opinion in important sections of the globe. *Carroll Binder. Annals of the American Academy. Jl.* '37. *p.* 44.

I have felt, that I should modify my position some-what on the question of a large navy, at least to the extent that I feel bound to keep our country armed to an extent greater than Japan is armed or greater than either Italy or Germany is armed. I believe, however, that the plan now proposed in America contemplates an armament unreasonably large and unnecessary.

I think there would be little chance for Japan to make any headway against our navy at present, but she is increasing hers and building battleships greater than any now in existence. She does not need them except for conquest. A combination of nations such as Japan, Italy and Germany might well change the map of Europe almost overnight.

To me it seems almost as if these nations have gone wild and have lost all sense of decency and honor. Bombs are being dropped upon civilians and upon women and children and those who are not bearing arms are the ones who apparently must suffer and die. If we are living in that kind of a world, then it seems to me, no matter how we feel or what we think, we must make reasonable preparations, at least, to meet such a contingency. *Senator George W. Norris. New York Times. Mr.* 28, '38. *p. 2.*

Mr. Hull has pursued a consistent middle course. He knows that an appearance of weakness invites trouble; he knows that even if a government has washed its hands of its citizens, nevertheless if those citizens get into trouble, the American public would clamor for their protection and no government would absolve itself of this obligation. On the other hand, he knows that the vast majority of our citizens do not wish to take part in means of pressure.

So the American government has followed a middle road: it has protected its citizens and its rights vigorously, stanchly and consistently; it has used a tone which is both resolute and friendly.

There are people in our country who believe that we would under no circumstance go to war; there are also people who believe that our participation in any major conflict is inevitable. Neither of them can be sure of their assertion. The development of history alone will show which of them is right.

I know there are some things our nation would fight for. I believe there is a policy under wise leadership to keep the United States out of a great struggle. I admit the danger of our being drawn in; I do not admit the inevitability. *Hugh R. Wilson, United States Ambassador to Germany. New York Times. Ap.* 14, '38. *p.* 14.

I recognize that all the dictatorships announce pacific intentions toward the rest of the world. I recognize that all of them insist that their armaments are either for defensive purposes or to give weight to their diplomacy in upholding what they conceive to be their just rights. But I recognize also that the same words may have different meanings to different persons or nations, and that "just rights" may have an elastic interpretation. We have seen, for instance, one country justify her operations in another country on the ground that her just rights in that territory were denied.

We have, then, a situation in which the great democracies, including our own, are living in the same world with powerful military autocracies. As realists we have to ask whether this fact means anything to us and whether our national policies should take it into the account.

* * *

The potential strength of the great peace-loving nations is the essential stabilizing influence in the world today. But the mere existence of this potential strength is not enough, as has been demonstrated. Take a common illustration. If policemen were under strict orders never under any circumstances to use force, how effective would they be in maintaining order? If a nation were similarly bound never to resort to any sort of force, economic or military, except in case of the actual invasion of its territory, how long would its rights be respected in an anarchistic world?

It is necessary, therefore, for us to continue to maintain our army and our navy, as strong and as efficient as the world situation warrants. They will not, of themselves, involve us in war, but by their existence they will render our peace more secure. *Harry H. Woodring. Address, May 5, 1938. Mimeo. p. 2, 4.*

Starting with a conviction that the chances that a new major war impends are so great as to force safeguard, I am in favor of a heavy armament program; this despite its obvious, known, and evil concomitants. Collective governmental efforts to postpone or wholly avert a major war, or to reduce the area within which inertia and desire for peace are indecently exploited, seem to me desirable. They seem to me, also, improbable of occurrence.

* * *

The totalitarian mobilization of the power of certain states brings home to a democracy three facts: (1) special jobs need specialized people—this cannot be ducked; (2) leeway to go right is also, and must be, leeway to go wrong—this cannot be ducked; (3) machinery for controlling officials stymies, and must stymie, needed action in any emergency—this cannot be ducked. To me, this means, indeed, some inevitable impingement of dictatorships on a democracy—if a democracy is to cope with the dictatorships—as ganged crooks inevitably impinge on police if police are to cope with ganged crooks.

In sum: for our own polity to survive, its movement must be toward *fighting power* (with the outrageous necessary costs and wastes); and, in international relations, the movement must be toward executive discretion (with the outrageous necessary costs and wastes).

But Mere People had better—and they can—gather themselves together speedily, and squeeze, and squeeze skillfully, and squeeze hard, to get the needed power and discretion *used*—and used *sensibly*. *Karl N. Llewellyn. Nation. Ap. 9, '38. p. 405.*

It may be taken for granted that we do not contemplate a war with Japan. Our possessions in the Pacific do not appear to make a war necessary. Japan does not need our small islands, having dozens of her own spread out in the Pacific. The Philippines are on the way to independence.

But with Japan riding hard and fast behind its militarists in China, it would be unwise policy for the United States to act on the theory that we contemplate no clash with Nippon. It is only as Russia, Britain, and the United States assert themselves with firmness as to Far Eastern rights and interests that Japan's military expansionists are likely to respect any limits to their reckless invasion of China and to their cool disregard of the interests of other Powers.

Aside from Japan, South and Central America represent a vital factor in our naval policy. Fascist nations such as Germany and Italy are seeking increasing footholds on the Western Hemisphere. Airplane routes are being established. Rapid expansion is taking place in their trade volume. In Fascist policy, military, political and economic programs are one.

The Monroe Doctrine is not beyond challenge in this situation. The prestige of the United States depends almost entirely upon its military readiness, in the eyes of militaristic Germany and Italy. It is quite clear from

Mussolini's respect for Britain in the Mediterranean, and Hitler's heeding of warning from France and Russia, that armed preparedness on the part of non-Fascist nations has had restraining effect. *Hartford Times. Quoted in Current History. Ap. '38. p. 32.*

With actual and threatened conflicts shattering or endangering the peace of at least one-fourth of the people of the world, American citizens are naturally concerned for our own peace and security. While the War Department is not charged with the conduct of foreign affairs, this branch of the administration, together with the navy, has the responsibility for the defense of the country against attack from any quarter. In an uneasy world, made restless by actual or potential warfare, ordinary prudence suggests that we look to our defenses. While our nation has no thought of aggression our people very properly expect that our territory shall be protected against the aggression of others.

I am happy to report that the United States Army is now more efficient than at any time in its peacetime history. . . . Nevertheless, in spite of these advances, the United States army is relatively weaker, compared with armies of other great countries, than it was a year ago. This is due to the fact that most of the other major powers have increased the size of their armies and have materially improved their equipment. In the case of several leading countries many thousand reservists have been placed on prolonged active duty because of actual or threatened hostilities. Increases in armaments have gone forward at an enormous rate. Practically every important nation has greatly increased its budget for military expenditures.

I certainly do not recommend that the United States join in this feverish arms race. Our national policy is wholly defensive and it would be highly undesirable for us to maintain at enormous expense a huge standing army, or any force larger than necessary to protect our homeland and possessions. However, I do think as insurance against attack we should further strengthen our armed forces. *Annual Report of the Secretary of War, 1937. p.* 1-2.

There is a strong school of opinion, both in Congress and in the country, which believes that the United States should take no step at this time to strengthen its own armaments and make no move to uphold its rights in any part of the world beyond our frontiers. Those who favor this course of action would have the American government throw overboard not only its own nationals abroad, and the properties which they have acquired by legitimate means for lawful ends, but also the traditional interest of this country in the principle of open markets for world trade and its still more fundamental interest in the maintenance of orderly processes of international law. But would such a policy as this, a policy of retreat and withdrawal, actually enable us to avoid the risks of war? There is no good reason to think so. On the contrary, there is every reason to believe that, by choosing to remain weak in the face of other nations' armaments and by waiving all question of respect for American interests, in whatever quarter of the world these interests may be challenged, we should merely invite further "acts of depredation" which would in the long run be bound to inflame American opinion to such a degree that war would be inevitable.

The best alternate to this willingness to gamble on the intentions of other nations is a strengthening of our own armaments, until such time as it is possible once more to consider methods of international limitation, and a calm but firm insistence on the observance of our rights. These are the present policies of the Roosevelt Administration. They are aimed at peace, not war; at the prevention of incidents which may lead to war; at

strengthening this country's hand, so that its influence
may count more heavily on the side of that decent respect for international obligations which alone can bring
peace and order. *Editorial. New York Times. Ja.* 29,
'38. *p.* 14.

Do not imagine that fascism will sweep over the
world without touching America; every country contains
morbid elements that will gladly harbor this disease,
just as every individual has weaknesses which may, if
uncorrected by treatment or happy circumstances, lead
him into a prison or an asylum for the insane. Still
less must one fancy 'nat the nightmare that now confronts us will disar pear if we close our eyes tightly
and smile propitiatory smiles—that is the behavior of
children. Unfortunately, the present world is not fit
for children to live in; fascists delight to drop bombs
on their heads. Thousands of men are now in concentration camps who kept on "hoping that time would
change things." Time changes nothing; men must act.

*   *   *

To implement non-intercourse we must take risks.
We have no guarantee against fascist piracy even in
times of peace; our shipping might have to be placed
on a war basis to avoid such typical barbarian attacks.
And further to strengthen our hand, we should—in contradiction to our present policy of "neutrality"—build
up a navy capable of keeping the sea-lanes open in
peace and war for the passage of goods to non-fascist
countries. I make no effort to gloze in pacifist terms
the assumptions of this policy; the axiom on which it
is based is that *fascism has already declared war.*
Fascism is a vicious force that now seriously threatens
American democracy, and to defend ourselves and our
institutions we must take the initiative, before it has
consolidated its power, before it has further undermined

our self-confidence, before its successful depredations
have increased its capacities for conquest. If that means
war, it means war only as an alternative to something
far more brutal and disastrous than war—submission
to fascism itself. *Lewis Mumford. New Republic.
My.* 18, '38. *p.* 40-1.

Every driver of a car knows the importance of gas
and oil stations along the roads. For the navy, the
base and supply question is not so simple. Naval bases
must have large stores of fuel, 4,500 tons for one
filling of a single battleship; food in great quantity, a
carload daily for the battleship force alone; reserve
ammunition, 12 tons for ⁀ single salvo; besides docking and repair facilities and material, and defenses
against hostile raiding. We have bases on both coasts,
in the Hawaiian Islands and in the Canal Zone. They
would be taxed to the utmost. We have also footholds
in the West Indies, Guam, Samoa and the Philippines.
To equip and defend them as operating supports would
be a heavy task. Wise foresight would fully prepare
them in time of peace; no threat to any nation. Great
Britain followed that course, the world map being dotted
all over with her supporting points. For lack of them
our cruisers must have a long cruising radius, with armament and speed enough to take care of themselves
when alone. These factors neccessitate large size and
heavy guns for American cruisers.

To keep the operatng bases supplied requires many
merchant vessels, which must be guarded while making
passage. Unless in good condition, manned by loyal
Americans and of modern construction and speed, naval
operations will be greatly hindered.

The fleet itself comprises battleships, cruisers, destroyers, submarines, aircraft and their carriers, mine
vessels and tenders, besides merchant vessels as auxiliaries. The battleship is the backbone of the fleet.

Without these heavy-weights naval effort could be dissipated by a navy which had them. For force of any kind there must be strong backbone. Severe punishment can be taken by a battleship—and keep on fighting. Torpedoes are a serious danger. In the World war no group of ships, no battleship nor cruiser, ever went to sea without a guard of destroyers, to screen against submarines. Yet torpedo damage is not necessarily fatal. In the Battle of Jutland, the battleship Marlborough, tho heavily damaged by a torpedo, kept her place in the battle line at seventeen knots for eight hours, until ordered into port, which was reached in safety. *Admiral Reginald R. Belknap. Vital Speeches. Ap.* 1, '38. *p.* 358.

Such a neutrality as is advocated by the American isolationists has been Hitler's greatest hope. He rejects collective security. Instead of wanting to have all countries guarantee the peace, he urges that when hostilities break out between two states "the other nations withdraw at once from both sides." Hitler insists on the "localizing of smaller conflicts." He regards this as the essence of complete neutrality. Only the aggressor and the attacked fight. The others sit and watch. Germany marches into Czechoslovakia. Russia, France, and England remain neutral. Germany wins the war. Next Germany violates Poland. The powers maintain an Olympic passivity. France's turn would be next and then England's. Neutrality followed to its natural and logical conclusion means the end of international law and the collapse of diplomacy. It is wind in the sails of aggressors.

Hitler advocates neutrality because he wants to pave his way to military victory. And American pacifists advocate neutrality because they do not understand this and the other realities of the world situation. They

see the formal side and think there is nothing more
to it. They think neutrality will keep us out of war.

* * *

Early in January France was frightened by suspi-
cious German activity in Morocco. Paris rapped on
the table, rapped hard, and within twenty-four hours
Hitler made a statement disavowing any intention of
digging himself into Morocco. Today France may be
poised for similar decisiveness in the whole Spanish
problem. Germany and Italy have already sent to Spain
too many troops for the comfort of the French People's
Front. France will not act without Britain. This
means that it will have to overcome English obstructions.
But if both countries do move against Italian-German
aggression in Spain, they can end the civil war soon.
Similar situations would arise very seldom for the
United States, but an unneutral America could, without
moving a single man or gun, work for peace and social
progress. *Nation. F.* 20, '37. *p.* 200.

The American Legion is composed of men, many
of whom learned by bitter experience what it meant
to enter a great war unprepared. Many of these men
learned what it meant to be armed with foreign-made
rifles, equipped with foreign-made machine guns—to
bear American-made materials only at the conclusion
of the World war and, in many instances, after the
armistice.

The Legion demands, therefore, that in the air and
on the land this nation be equipped so that the agony
of sending unprepared youths to war may be avoided
if ever again a national emergency calls the men of
America to the colors.

The Legion does not demand a gigantic army. It
does not demand an army as large as the forces of

the smallest countries in Europe.   But it asks that the
small professional armed forces of America be thoroly
equipped with the most modern implements of war,
that they be trained as experts, the schooling force for
any citizen army that may be called upon to leave home
and plow to save the nation.

The Legion asks that the air forces of the army
and the navy be so manned and equipped, that this
country can maintain superiority in the air above its
lands and possessions and its men in the field, if ever
called upon to do so.   They want this, too, without any
question of a doubt.   Over its own people, its own
lands, and its own armies, wherever they must fight,
the Legion demands that America must rule the air.

The Legion sponsors the enlargement of the National
Guard and its proper training.   It stands behind the
continued development of the Organized Reserves.   It
calls for no check in the military training in the Reserve Officers Training Corps of the land-grant colleges.
It says that no youth is injured if he discovers at an
early age that he has an obligation to his country.   The
Legion knows that no militarist is made out of the
youth who learns to stand at attention, to carry himself
as a man and a soldier, to obey commands, and to
equip himself to give commands.   *Capt. Robert Allen
Griffin. American Legion, Dept. of California. Congressional Record. Ap. 12, '38. p. 6988.*

There remains one alternative policy, which may be
both more rational in itself and a more comprehensible
interrelation of political and naval policy.

That is the perhaps lamentable but very practical
fact that the navy is the amplifier of the voice of the
diplomat.   His voice speaks exactly as loud as the potential voice of his cannon.   If these cannon are potentially loud enough, they do not need to speak.   The
voice of reason will be heard and heeded.   Therefore,

because America has diplomatic messages which it wishes heard, notably in the Far East, it may need the necessary amplifier to make its words audible—and audited. If this sounds cynical, consider some actual instances.

Why is Japan a major power and China a secondary one, in the family of nations? Not by reason merely of the fine quality and high culture of both peoples. Both have these qualifications and China has had them longer. Not the importance of their lands and products. Both are important. But Japan has an army and a navy. Therefore its diplomats are heard. When China undertook to scrap treaties, it was bluntly warned not to do it. When Japan openly flouted them, the protest was mild and the action nil. When Germany, disarmed, protested against impossible exactions, they were nevertheless insisted on. When Germany, rearmed, refused to respect any treaties, everybody yielded. When Greece and Bulgaria undertook illegal war, their heads were knocked together and they were commanded to obey the law. When Italy, armed and threatening, defied the law of nations, it was gently chided. If Britain, which was able, if it had been willing to pay the cost, to compel compliance, had spoken with a sterner voice, it would have been heard and would not have had to fight to enforce its will.

If, then, we propose that in the future the voice of our diplomats shall again be raised across the Pacific, to insist with irrefutable arguments on peace, the sanctity of treaties, and the inviolability of the sovereignty of others, we know that mere reason will not be enough. We have that reason now, and we are not even listened to. With a loud enough megaphone, the voice of reason will be heard. *Chester H. Rowell. Amerasia. Mr. '37. p. 8.*

Peace-at-any-price groups in the larger democratic countries have been so very active that the militaristic and intensely nationalistic countries have come to the mistaken belief that all democracies are becoming peace-at-any-price nations.

Some militaristic nations take full advantage of the situation and proceed to tear up treaties and break international law whenever it suits them to do so, and to take by force, if they can, what they think they need. With cold-blooded calculation, these nations have counted upon the love of peace in democracies to save them from punishment for their wrongdoing. They will continue to go as far as they can until some kind of force stops them.

Recognizing only force, these autocratic governments lose much respect for peace-loving democracies. Our friendliness they mistake for softness.

The more peace-at-any-price propaganda is carried on in democracies, the more the dictator nations will disregard international law and morality and human rights, because the greater the nonresistance the less chance of punishment for their wrongdoing.

Democracies, if they will prevent the onward rush of international anarchy of brute force, must show the firmness and strength of character that they really do possess. They have firmness, but they must develop more firmness. They are not as soft as they appear to be. But they are too soft.

Strength, manhood, firmness are not unchristian. They are not traits of war. They are the only traits of peace that are effective among a family of nations where there is no effective international law. Fear does not make for peace. But courage does.

Force can be applied to a recalcitrant nation by peace-loving nations without necessarily fighting. Various economic moves can be made. Supplies, arms and credits can be given to the weak nation that is attacked by the aggressor nation.

Mr. Hull is navigator of our ship of state in the dangerous sea of foreign relations. He must steer us safely thru that sea which abounds with rocks and shoals. Don't rock the boat. Don't throw monkey wrenches into the machinery. For the moment, at least, trust your navigator. It is no time for destructive criticism. *Richard E. Byrd. Literary Digest. F.* 12, '38. *p.* 16-17.

The philosophy of non-resistant pacifism has displayed all of its wares, it has used up all of its theorizings, and today it is not only bankrupt but there are good reasons for believing that the verdict of history will place upon it the blame for many of the shocking international crimes committed in the past decade.

A very recent letter from a solid, substantial English friend, a man of profoundly pacific attitude, in explaining why Great Britain so decidedly let us down in a concert of action which almost certainly would have checked Japan in Manchuria, says that the pacifist sentiment of the time had tied the hands of the government so tightly that positive and vigorous action was impossible.

There may have been other factors in that situation, but the negative force of pacifist idealism was certainly a prominent ingredient in the mess then brewing, which has since produced the rape of Ethiopia, the Italian venture in Spain and the present terrible slaughter of thousands of Chinese.

All law has as its only firm foundation the ultimate appeal to force to compel obedience. All the way from a city or village ordinance as to the proper places for parking cars clear up to international affairs, the laws are useless unless they are to be respected and if need be enforced.

Only the events of the past few months have enabled me to see that fact clearly. A year ago I said that all the American holdings in China were not worth a single month of fighting for their protection. So far as the money is concerned that is still the case. But something more than money is at stake. Every scrap of international law, every prospect of a future peaceful, law-abiding world is at stake today.

Law-abiding Americans should find in their flag a symbol of the protecting power of a mighty people wherever they go. We ought to keep the law honestly ourselves and we must insist, by overwhelming force if that is needed, that others shall not reduce the whole fabric of international law to a mass of wreckage. Any other policy leads us directly from little troubles into big ones.

Theodore Roosevelt was right. Uncle Sam should "speak softly and carry a big stick." The stick should be carried in plain view and it ought to be very large and convincing. This is especially true if we are to maintain a policy of isolation. If we can come to a time when the great powers, including ourselves, can agree to take common action against any nation whose armed soldiers trespass by a single inch across the boundaries of another country, we may be able to diminish the size of the big stick, but not until then. *Elbert H. Clarke. New York Times. Ja.* 16, '38. *Sec.* 4. *p.* 9.

Recent events are staring us straight in the face, and it is incumbent upon us to shape our course in such fashion as to make this generation of Americans and future generations in this country safe against this force. So long as this bitter thing goes on, I insist that America must be able to defend herself. The cost of defense, of adequate and successful defense, is infinitely less than the cost of failure and defeat.

I think it can be said that the Japanese aggressions in China are due fundamentally to the pressure of population in the Japanese islands, an industrial population seeking an outlet.

We may not like the methods, but it is not the first time in the history of the world that such things have happened; and if Middle Europe is to be united under one government, dictatorial in character, not hesitating to use force in seeking outlets, expansions for its people, we shall see another example of what is now going on in China, except on a much larger scale; and we shall not be the master of that event.

We have elected, wisely, I think, to stay out of it all; but eventually expansion of peoples, led by dictators believing in the exercise of force in the achievement of their aims, will reach the Western Hemisphere.

I look upon this [Naval Construction] bill as representing a realization of that grim, grim fact, as an indication that we are learning that we must be masters of our own destiny.

The history of nations shows upon innumerable occasions that the defense of a people may have to be carried on 1,000 miles from their homes, or 5,000 miles from their homes. Our children and grandchildren may live to see the day in which in its own defense, America, off the coast of Brazil, may fight the first naval battle of a war brought against her by an aggressor.

That would be just as truly an act and battle of defense as if it were fought in the Narrows of New York Harbor. Unless I misjudge things, I cannot escape the conclusion that our navy must be strong enough to protect this hemisphere. No one else is going to protect it for us. We do not ask anybody to do it for us.

In order to do that, we have got to have a strong navy; in fact, a stronger navy than we have now, and stronger even than the navy already authorized. *Representative James W. Wadsworth. New York Times. Mr. 16, '38. p. 13.*

In view of recent developments in Asia, it seems tolerably clear that if this nation is again obliged to enter into armed conflict with any other, and to defend itself against aggression, the attack will come, not across the Atlantic, but across the Pacific. And for any attack coming across the Pacific aimed at our shores, if we hold possession—actual, fortified, defensive possession— of the coast as well as the main body of Alaska, we shall necessarily be in control of the interior, short line from the Orient, and will thus be in the strongest possible position for the defense of both Alaska and of the continental United States. But if possession of Alaska be in the hands of an enemy, that enemy will occupy the most advantageous post to carry out offensive operations against the United States. Nothing is clearer, nothing more certain than the proposition, which is based upon the elementary principles of military and naval art, that possession in force of the short, interior line always gives strategic and actual control.

The Territory of Alaska at the present time has no defensive forces whatsoever, with the exception of 300 infantry stationed at Chilkoot Barracks and approximately six naval airplanes which are located at Sitka, both in southeastern Alaska. In the event of hostilities in that area, our military and naval forces now in Alaska would be obliged to escape or surrender. They are not large enough to fight.

Yes, the possession of Alaska by foreign and hostile nationals would be a constant source of menace to the peace and safety of the United States. And this is true because of something not known when Alaska was purchased from Russia in 1867. Just as the invention of gunpowder destroyed feudalism, so the invention and development of the airplane has set at naught the former earthbound concepts of military and naval strategy. A few years ago Great Britain felt perfectly safe because the Straits of Dover, and the English Channel, and the North Sea, intervene between the British Isles and continental Europe. But only the other day, in the British House of Commons, former Prime Minister Baldwin made a statement which no one can doubt, that the defense line of Great Britain is no longer at the Channel, but on the Rhine. The modern military airplanes can exercise their terrible striking power hundreds of miles away from their bases within the nation. And so if the defense line of England is no longer at the Channel but on the Rhine, then it is certain that the defense line of the United States is not on the actual shores of our Atlantic or Pacific or Gulf coasts, but a long, long distance farther away out in the oceans which wash those shores. *Representative Anthony J. Dimond. Congressional Record. My. 12, '38. p. 8998.*

Were one to draw upon the charts of the world a line down the middle of the Atlantic, firmly drawn until it tapers off into uncertainty where Brazil thrusts out toward Africa, and, in the Pacific, another line, starting lightly in the storm-defended Aleutians, then sweeping firmly south some thousand miles west of Hawaii and again tapering off into the no man's land of the south Pacific, these two lines would enclose our sphere of strategic control. Within them lies the hemisphere which fate has given to us as our empire of destiny. History, geography, and economics combine in fixing as ours this imperium of the two Americas. If, and only if, we maintain our present naval strength, no enemy can drive our fleet or our merchantmen from the seas. Here no single foe can deny economic self-sufficiency to an adequately armed America. Should war ever shut the distant seas against us, here we can still live, a nation prosperous and powerful. Here is our zone of defense. Beyond it lie those unpredictable sea areas where the future may yet summon our arms to terminate by offensive operations a war which only aggression can thrust upon us.

Surveying the troubled world of today, chaotic Europe, the insecure Channel, the crowded Mediterranean, the racket-ridden Orient, we may well rejoice that here in the west under our guns lies the world's most complete and defensive military base, the arsenal of two sister continents. To use well and to guard well these vast resources, such must be our future. Surely in no other age and to no other people has fate more clearly dictated the lines of national policy.

Production, trade, and shipping all are elements of the national economic strength and independence which give ability honorably to maintain neutrality or victoriously to participate in war. It is a fact, and it is useless sentimentally to bemoan it, that the industrial forces which so amply sustain life today are the forces whose politically fostered competition may lead to hostilities and themselves become the most ready and effective weapons for the destruction of the very life they sustain. That is the paradox of modern industrial civilization which leads some gloomy philosophers to believe that it contains within itself the germs of self-destruction. Be that as it may, the economic factors cannot be neglected by those whose sole duty it is to prepare for security at sea. Our nation, above all others, stands invulnerable to blockade. For us alone the prosecution of hostilities need not be haunted by the dread that the stoppage of vital imports will mean industrial starvation at home. Adequately armed afloat as we soon shall be, granted there is no startling increase in foreign fleets, we can rest secure here within our own strategic zone. Here we need not fear the power of any adversary, but, should the call ever come again, we can throw the full might of our matchless economy toward offensive and victorious war. *Lieutenant Commander Melvin F. Talbot. United States Naval Institute Proceedings. O. '37.*

To the average person the term "national defense" means soldiers and battleships and fighting planes, but it has a far deeper meaning in these times. Modern war is something more than the mere impact of men; we learned that during the World war. In time of war the nation is fighting for its very life, and every resource and every effort must be thrown into the struggle to bring victory with the least possible loss of lives and resources. The nation must have not only men and ships and airplanes, but it must have a quick and steady source of supplies both for the fighting forces and the civilian population. This means industrial mobilization.

Until recent years the United States has lagged behind other nations in the matter of national defense. At last we are building toward the minimum needs of defense from a military and naval standpoint. This will not suffice, however, unless we have industrial preparedness at the same time. This does not mean military supervision of our industries or the regimentation of our factories in time of peace; it does not mean the slightest distrubance to industry or business or finance as long as peace is maintained.

Industrial preparedness means the setting up of a plan, and authorization for the President of the United States to put that plan into effect by force of law when war is declared, or in time of emergency preceding a declaration of war. Under this plan the President would be authorized to bring into the service of the country, in time of war, capital, industry, resources, services, and manpower, with special privileges or profit for none; and to use them for the national defense and common welfare during the period of the war emergency.

When war comes we must have an army, navy, and air corps to protect us on land, at sea, and in the air. Our combat forces must be supplied with guns, ships, airplanes, ammunition, shoes, clothing, and the hundreds of other things which are vital to a fighting force in modern war. Similarly our civilian population, which becomes literally a vast service of supplies behind the lines, must be properly housed, well fed, adequately clothed, and provided with all of the customary comforts that are possible. And for combatants and noncombatants alike, these things must be obtained at reasonable prices if we are to avoid the mistakes of the past which have plunged the country into debt and economic disaster following war.

In America we have a vast industrial power, as potent a fighting force as any army or navy. If we have a law which will put this tremendous power into instantaneous operation for war service, it is doubtful that any nation will dare attack us; and if one should, we would be prepared to meet and stop its force quickly, efficiently, and economically. Bernard M. Baruch, chairman of the War Industries Board, has declared that such a law "will be more of a protection to this country than a standing army of a million men." If we had been thus ready to fight, it is questionable whether we would have been forced into the World war. *American Legion. In Report of the Committee on Military Affairs on S. 25. 75th Cong. 1st Sess. Senate Report. No. 480. May 6, '37. p. 4-5.*

A navy is an instrument for the achievement of a definite national purpose, and I have already stated to you our naval policy. To repeat, it is for the maintenance of peace, and to insure our national security. The United States lies across an impressive portion of the North American continent. The shoreline from Maine around to Brownsville, Texas; and from San Diego up to British Columbia, is 21,862 statute miles. The vast territory of Alaska, measured along the tidal shoreline, adds to this figure 15,312 miles. The energies of our people have not been confined to our continental limits. In the way of insular possessions, our flag flies over the Virgin Islands and Puerto Rico, comparatively close at hand. Further away, but as vital to our system of transportation and internal communication, is the Panama Canal, its Atlantic entrance 1,974 sea miles from New York; its Pacific mouth 3,249 miles from San Francisco. Westward from San Francisco 2,091 miles, lie the Hawaiian Islands. Our sea-road leads still westward to Guam, 5,053 miles from California; and to the Philippines, 6,221 miles from our shores; and, while we have set up the beginnings of an autonomous government in the Philippines, under the present laws we cannot lay down our obligations there for another ten years.

Along our extended coasts our domestic maritime trade proceeds with great regularity, ranging from comparatively small vessels voyaging between nearby ports, to the great ocean liners that travel from California to New York thru the Panama Canal. Our merchant ships go out to our islands, and to all the world, carrying our citizens and their goods. For the security of all this coastline, for the Delaware capes, and the sandy beaches of the Gulf, and for the western headlands, and for the great and vital artery across Panama, and for the long sea-highway that stretches across the Pacific, the navy has a real and definite responsibility.

We have what amounts to a maritime empire. It is idle here to discuss how we got it; impractical, in this disordered world, to look into the future. As a sensible people, we must deal with the present. To preserve the integrity of these shores that sprawl from the Arctic Circle to the Tropic Zone, and to protect the flow of legitimate traffic between our seaports and our possessions across the seas, we must have ample sea power, a necessary requisite of which is an adequate navy.

Let us face conditions as they stand today. The lessons of sea power are written plain for all to read on the pages of history. It was the sea power of the ancient Greeks, rising under the menace of the Persian Empire, that broke their enemies and established the security of their home territories and their colonies across the seas. Salamis is one of the great names. Sea power won for the Romans their long war with Carthage; and sea power for centuries maintained the peace of Rome around the known world. Behind the galleys came the legions, and behind the legions, the traders; and while Rome continued vigorous enough to maintain her land forces and her sea forces, she ruled the earth, and laid the foundations of the modern world. In the middle ages, it was sea power that set up the Spanish colonies, and brought the plate fleets to Spanish harbors, laden with gold and silver ingots out of Peru and Mexico; and it was a new sea power, emerging from the fierce energies of Elizabethan England, that planted in the new world the colonies out of which our nation sprang. *Assistant Secretary of the Navy H. L. Roosevelt. Vital Speeches. D. 16, '35. p. 180.*

NEGATIVE DISCUSSION

ARMAMENTS ARE FOREIGN POLICY [1]

What policies are possible? First of all there is the policy implicit and explicit in President Roosevelt's speech in Chicago last October, the policy of quarantine. Unless he was just talking thoughtlessly or was bluffing, he believes that the United States should pass judgment on all the quarrels in Europe and Asia, quarantine the "wicked," and employ the army and navy of the United States in making good the quarantine when it is defied. This policy calls for big battleships to be used in aggressive warfare in the Far Pacific or the Far Atlantic. It is true that many naval officers doubt the utility of battleships for any kind of warfare, but, if they have any utility, it is for aggressive mass action. Between 1895 and 1914 the German Imperial Government built battleships instead of submarines and airplanes and thus helped to defeat itself; yet there are naval officers, both quarterdeck and swivel-chair admirals, who insist on having dreadnaught monsters.

The other foreign policy for the United States is that of abstaining from the quarrels of Europe and Asia, avoiding all gratuitous advice and insults to foreign governments, and defending the continental home of the United States and the adjacent waters. This policy calls for a different division of funds between the army and the navy. The idea of Germany, Italy, or Japan sending a fleet of battleships conveying 500,000 soldiers across the seas in majestic array is

[1] From statement presented to the House Naval Affairs Committee by Charles A. Beard, February 9, 1938.

simply fantastic—the kind of nightmare which a holder of shipbuilding stocks has when ordinary business is bad. Furthermore, despite all the emphasis on the utility of the navy for offensive wars in European or Asiatic waters, it is the army that will have to do the real fighting if anything is to be gained. If Congress votes the President's naval program it should triple the appropriations for the army in order to put any real sense into it.

If the Congress of the United States actually intends to adopt the policy of lecturing nations in Europe and Asia and making its lessons good by arms, then it should probe the President's program to the bottom and find out what fighting gear is necessary to carry it out. If on the other hand, Congress intends to provide defense for the American domain of interest in this hemisphere, it should make corresponding alterations in the President's program, redivide funds between the army and the navy, and redistribute the funds among suitable types of fighting craft for the navy.

But we are told that the fascist goblins of Europe are about to take South America, that Mussolini will march in seven league boots across the Atlantic, thru the straits of Gibraltar, to Brazil, or that Hitler or the Mikado will do it some other way. This is the new racket created to herd the American people into President Roosevelt's quarantine camp. All that Congress needs to do to satisfy itself on this point is to call naval officers into a secret session, vote them a retiring allowance so that the executive ax may not fall upon them, and ask them just how Hitler or Mussolini or the Mikado can perform this water-crossing miracle now, with our present defenses. It is high time that members of Congress may enlighten themselves on this point by reading the testimony of naval officers on previous bills and especially on the London naval treaty.

But the cry goes up: "Are we to leave American citizens without protection in China?" To this question there are two answers. The first is that if we had a navy twice as big as that proposed by President Roosevelt, it could not alone impose victory on Japan in Far Eastern waters. Certainly even with such aid as Great Britain might, could, or should render, when, as, and if, the American navy contemplated by the President's program would run into mortal hazards in any effort to impose victory on the Japanese navy in its own waters, the navy for which the President asks cannot give American citizens the protection of superior force.

The second answer to this question in respect of protection involves an analysis. Who is to be protected? Where? And in doing what? On these points we are bound by somewhat settled law and practice, in which the United States has concurred. Even the State Department would not claim that American citizens have a right to go sight-seeing on the battlefields where the Japanese and Chinese armies are fighting. Nor do Americans anywhere have the "right" to insist on doing business as usual in war zones on land or sea, that is, a right in defense of which American soldiers and sailors must die. During the unhappy Civil War in the United States the federal government did not assure protection to foreigners who wished to travel in the war zones of the South. Nor did it apologize to foreign governments when any of their nationals got hurt in attempting to do so. Nor did it compensate foreigners for their "losses" in Confederate trade, loans, or bonds.

A war is raging in China, whether the fact is admitted or not, and the place for American citizens is out of these foreign war zones. As the late Admiral Sims declared in 1935, the army and navy of the United States must not be employed to protect the profits of traders in war-infested regions abroad. Their duty is fulfilled in assisting in the evacuation of American citizens and their movable property from the war zones. This is not to "scuttle and run." It is to follow settled international practice and the dictates of prudence. No such naval program as the President demands is required by such practice or prudence. And according to realistic knowledge that can be gained from a study of sea warfare, the navy for which he asks could not assure the protection of these fictitious rights against the naval force of Japan. Either way, his program is clouded with doubts.

When minutely analyzed, when placed squarely in the history of sea power, when studied in relation to the present posture of the sea powers in their separate strategic areas, the President's program has no meaning save as one step in the direction of applying his quarantine doctrine to Europe and Asia. Next year Congress will be called upon to take the next step. So the whole business boils down to a single issue: Do the American people and the Congress that is supposed to represent them want to commit themselves to the entangled obligations which the quarantine doctrine involves? The hour of a fateful decision has arrived.

Before Congress makes the decision, it will do well to heed the warning of Admiral Sims on the crucial issue of battleships: "Submarines and airplans have clipped the wings of seapower and the best thing to do with our battleships in case of an attack upon our coasts would be to send them as far as possible up the Mississippi River." This disposes of the President's contention that his program is for the defense of our coasts and also of the implication that they would be effective in attacks on Japanese coasts. In the light of such expert and disinterested evidence, Congress should make its decision.

PREPAREDNESS FOR PEACE [2]

Can another holocaust be averted?   Can another world war, which would make the last one seem like a skirmish, be avoided? I answer:

Yes. Provided there is swift, sure, intelligent action. Provided we turn our attention now to a vigorous preparation for peace. Provided we use a fraction of the thought, planning, energy and money we spend preparing for war, in rebuilding friendly international relations. Provided we strengthen every possible factor in opposition to those forces that would involve us in another nation's quarrels.

Our first task is to recognize clearly those forces that are drawing the nations relentlessly toward war. We do but waste our efforts if we do not see plainly our problems. I dare to enumerate what are the outstanding causes of the present war preparations, which must be recognized and dealt with before a program of peace building can be effective:

There is the desire on the part of some nations for "expansion"—outlets for their crowded populations, for raw materials, for colonies.

Commercial rivalries—the fight for supremacy in trade and commerce.

The selfish nationalistic spirit finding its expression in secret diplomacies, treaties and intrigues, those breeders of fear and suspicion that always have led to war.

The desire of dictatorial leaders of some nations to spread their political doctrines over the world. And their desire to cover up their own failures, blunderings and weaknesses by causing their peoples to concentrate energies and efforts upon a common cause of war against others.

The repeated failures of disarmament conferences, building in minds thruout the world the suspicion that "some other nation" is responsible and must be dealt with by war.

The building of huge armaments, the unrestricted advancement of war preparations themselves, all over the world.

[2] From article by Gerald P. Nye, United States Senator from North Dakota. *Christian Science Monitor Weekly Magazine Section.* March 10, 1937. p. 2.

These things, I maintain, are barriers across the highway to world amity. We need a straightforward, continuous program of peace preparation to deal with them, to overcome their disastrous effects.

The United States has chosen to join the scramble of big military preparations. Our expenditures for war preparedness this year will run well over $1,000,000,000! Other nations are doing likewise. Yet we wonder why international hatreds are kept alive and only overt acts are needed to touch off the powder kegs. I remain a believer in a national defense capable of repulsing the attack of any possible enemy of my country. But I offer as an example of the effect this frantic rivalry for military power must produce upon the nations, the words of a friend who wrote:

> I have a neighbor with whom I wish to be a friend. He also wants to be a friend of mine, and we both agree that we must get along peacefully together. In order to show him my good intentions I built a high, barbed-wire fence, with steel pickets, between his house and mine. He, in turn, to convince me of his friendship, put a ferocious dog in his back yard. I then put bullet-proof glass in the window on his side and started wearing pistols in my belt. The other day I saw him moving supplies of poison gas and hand grenades into his house. Now I have a machine gun mounted in the front yard, and for the life of me I can't understand why we don't get along any better.

We need a conference to discuss disarmament, which will contain delegates genuinely interested in the cause of peace. Such conferences in the past have been made up of representatives whose interests are the same as those of the munitions plants which would lose business by disarmament, even in a small degree, and by delegates in gold braid, admirals and generals trained in the business of war and armament, not in peace and disarmament.

ARMAMENTS AND PEACE [3]

It is said that on the day when British Arms become formidable the ill-disposed states which are today hesitating whether to plunge into war will abandon the idea and definitely settle down to peace, from compulsion if not from choice. It may be so. It must be observed, none the less, that British armaments so far have been operating in precisely the opposite way. They were one of the causes of the Spanish war, which has now lasted more than a year, and of the war in China, which has just begun.

Why has Italy flung herself headlong into the Spanish conflict? Because for more than a year she has been living in terror of Britain's immense armaments. It is a universal terror, extending from the King and Mussolini to the mass of the populace, tho among the latter the fear is associated with a certain satisfaction and hope of liberation. But the government is in agitation and it has plunged into the Spanish affair because it hopes to strengthen its position in the Western Mediterranean against the contingency of a war with Britain. No doubt it plunged into the Spanish war in the belief that the enterprise was much simpler and easier than it has proved. Now that it is thus committed, it finds it very difficult to withdraw, and it maintains its intervention, torn between fear of Britain and the hope that Britain will not for the moment, and in the case of Spain, take any decisive action. Hence its perpetual vacillations.

The case of Japan is very similar. A personality well acquainted with the Far East assured me toward the end of 1936 that this year a new war between Japan and China would break out. "Japan," he said, "will profit by the present opportunity. She is satisfied that Great Britain, not being yet ready for action, will refrain

[3] By Professor Guglielmo Ferrero. *Spectator.* 159:452-3. September 17, 1937.

from interfering. In two or three years her plans might meet with far more formidable opposition or resistance." What does all this mean? It means that armaments are a two-edged weapon. They may ensure peace. They may equally precipitate war. For them to ensure peace, peaceably-minded governments must know how to use them—a difficult art, which the western world seems less and less able to master. To proclaim to the four corners of the compass, as Britain has been doing for the last year, "For the moment I shall do nothing because I am not ready, but only wait, and you will see what I shall be capable of doing in two years when I am armed"—to state the problem of peace thus before the world is to tell every ill-intentioned state to hurry up and take advantage of the moment. That is precisely what Italy and Japan have done. I should not be surprised if their example found imitators. Two years is a long time, and no one knows if even at the end of two years Britain will feel herself indisputably ready.

Japan has been equally encouraged by the law of neutrality adopted in the United States. This law, particularly as long as public opinion continues in its present mood, will be a solemn assurance given to all states tempted to misuse their force to the detriment of a weaker state that they can do what they like without fear of any move on America's part. We are living in strange times. It may be said broadly that from 1815 to 1914 the world enjoyed peace for a century, even if it did not live in a *régime* of perpetual peace. There were, it is true, wars in all continents, but they were few and almost all of them brief, and there was no difficulty in isolating and localising them. They did not form a chain of wars, one provoking another. That was a far better situation than we have to face today. But why was it that it was possible for peace to be maintained for a century as the normal condition in all countries? For the simple reason that every power feared, if it misused its strength, to find itself faced by a coalition. Bismarck himself was tortured by a nightmare of coalitions, and that was one of the reasons why he did not misuse his strength after 1870. It was a genuine collective security, tacitly accepted, unobtrusive. States organised it without saying so, and almost without realising it. It operated for a century over all continents with remarkable results.

Then comes 1914 and the outbreak of the World war. The world decides that everything the nineteenth century did is valueless, that something more and better is necessary, namely the organization of collective security, publicly, officially, juridically, diplomatically. Jurists trotted out theories which were to outlaw war and ensure perpetual peace. The League of Nations was planted on the shores of the Lake of Geneva, with an incredible number of typewriters and telephones at its disposal, charged with the mission of establishing the reign of law thruout the world. From that moment, every time a stronger state has attacked a weaker, everyone has made himself scarce and the weak has been left to the talons of the aggressor. China was deserted by everyone in 1931 and 1932, Abyssinia in 1936, Spain in 1937. China is now to be deserted again. The fear of coalitions, which was sufficient to secure to the whole world for a century a state of peace, if not actually permanent at any rate sufficiently stable, has become a fantastic bogy. Every state which contemplates a dastardly stroke derides it.

Such is the progress on which the world can pride itself as sequel to the World war, and thanks to the alleged rule of law established in 1919. In reality, in 1914 the lords and masters of the western world unchained violence, and, when the war was over, were no longer capable of chaining it up again. The whole world today runs the risk of falling into a situation like that in which Europe lived from 1797 to 1814. Wars followed one another like links in a chain, springing up successively after precarious truces, and all tracing their origin to a state of general fear. Without the Abyssinian war there would have been no Spanish war; without the Spanish war there would have been no Chinese war. The forging of the chain has begun, each war provoking another more serious.

It is imperative that public opinion in the great free countries should realize this situation, the most dangerous Europe has known since the beginning of the nineteenth century, for a resolute reversal of the policy of the great states is essential, and that will not be possible so long as public opinion in the great free countries remains convinced that to ensure peace it is sufficient to lavish the wealth of the world on armaments. The armaments may be completely useless, or even serve to provoke vast wars, if the policy of the states consists, whenever a war breaks out, in preserving peace by assuring to the most powerful state every facility for using and misusing its strength.

MORAL AND LEGAL BASES OF INTERNATIONAL PEACE [4]

What are the reasons for the change that has come over the relations of states during recent years? Why is it that the principles to which we pledged our faith in 1920 have failed to bring us the peace and security which we hoped to attain. It is not the principles that were at fault, for they were, so far as they went, the right principles. Rather the failure has been due to the fact that the principles were not given sufficiently wide application. Let us examine them together to see where the trouble lies.

The first of the great principles embodied in the Covenant of the League of Nations is the principle that

[4] From address of Charles G. Fenwick before the Institute of Public Affairs, University of Virginia, July 9, 1837.

no nation shall have any longer the right to be the judge in its own case. There is nothing new in this principle. It is part of the established law of the United States and of every other civilized state. It is not only the law of our individual states; it is the law of our federal government. In the United States the Supreme Court has jurisdiction over controversies between the member states of the Union, and it has handed down its decisions year after year in a wide variety of cases.

Why is it that the principle by which the collective judgment of the United States takes precedence over the judgment of the individual state of the Union has not been accepted as a basis for the settlement of international disputes? The answer is that it is the function of the courts to apply *existing law*. Beyond that they cannot go. If the existing law be inadequate, the remedy must be found elsewhere. No one can fairly criticize the numerous arbitration courts that have been set up from time to time by the nations; no one can fairly criticize the organization of the Permanent Court of International Justice or the character of the judges. But international courts have been unable to do more than to adjudicate claims on the basis of the *status quo*. The result is that the nations have been unwilling to entrust to them the really grave questions upon which peace or war may depend. Valuable as are the functions which international courts have to perform they must of necessity be limited to the lesser interests of states. It is the law that is at fault, not the courts.

The second of the great principles of law embodied in the Covenant of the League is the principle that the defense of nations is a collective responsibility of the whole group. The old right of self-help, the right to go to war whenever the individual nation felt that its interests called for measures of force is abolished. An attack upon one becomes an attack upon all and is met by the common action of all. Such is the system of collective security, and it also finds its parallel in the law of the individual state. Long ago the individual citizen lost the right to take the law into his own hands. It is to the community at large, acting through its executive officials, that the individual must look for his protection. The individual goes disarmed because the agents of the community are armed in his behalf. In like manner within the Union of the United States the individual state is disarmed by constitutional mandate; but it is disarmed only as a consequence of the prior assumption by the Union of the obligation to protect each of its members against invasion.

Why is it that the system of collective security established by the Covenant of the League has failed to meet the demands put upon it? The answer is not a difficult one. It is not merely because one of the leading powers has remained aloof from the League and thus weakened its collective character. It is not merely because several of the leading members of the League have defied its authority and taken the law into their own hands, altho such acts of lawlessness would have been difficult under any circumstances to control. It is rather because the Covenant itself was deficient in one fundamental respect. Law can be an agency of peace only if it undertakes to promote justice as well as to prevent violence. The framers of the Covenant put too much stress upon the prevention of violence, upon the maintenance of territorial boundaries and the existing status quo. They did not sufficiently realize that the League, if it was to be successful, must give equal attention to removing the causes of war and to promoting those conditions of social and economic life which are necessary to make law tolerable to those whom it attempts to control.

The failure of collective security has naturally been accompanied by the failure of efforts for the limitation of armaments. So long as the problem of the limitation of armaments is approached as a problem of ratios of relative individual national armaments, apart from any recognition of the collective responsibility of the whole community to protect each of its members, there is little probability of success in solving it. The record of the successive conferences of 1921, 1927 and 1930, should be sufficient proof of the futility of the method of reduction of armaments by ratio. Collective security must continue to be the condition precedent of effective disarmament; but it should be added that any degree of limitation would help to create an atmosphere in which plans of collective security might be more easily worked out.

PATRIOTISM [5]

The Senate investigation of munitions has brought to the munition-manufacturers a type of publicity which they do not desire. I know of no better way to describe the character of the arms-makers than by this little story. Once there was a little boy who was always trading with the other boys of his neighborhood. One time he decided he would sell a great many peashooters; so he got together one bunch of boys and told them that they needed protection against a gang of boys in another block, with whom they often had disputes. Our friends bought several shooters. Then our merchant quietly informed the other gang that their rivals were armed to the teeth, and quickly sold out his wares. Soon there was a fierce scrap between the two gangs, in which many a well-placed pea found its mark. Rocks and sticks began to fly, and most of the belligerents went home crying to mama and papa. Our vendor of the shooters had watched the whole fight—from a safe distance.

[5] By James Edwin Edwards, Student, George Washington Law School. *Social Science.* 11:332-4. October, 1936.

The arms-maker of today is that bad little boy grown up. But with him the problem is much more serious. In place of pea-shooters, he sells machine guns, poisonous gas, fighting 'planes, and heavy artillery. Instead of selling to neighborhood gangs, he sells to whole nations. He is no longer somewhat amusing. He is a merchant of death, profiteering on patriotism.

These grown-up bad boys stand before the high court of public opinion, convicted of crime against mankind.

The first charge against them is profiteering in human bloodshed. During the World War it cost, on an average, twenty-five thousand dollars to kill each soldier. Much of this blood-money went into the pockets of the arms-makers. The dividends of death are tremendous. For example, Skoda, which exports forty per cent of its production, paid a dividend of 28½ per cent in the comparatively peaceful year of 1930. In this country the Dupont Company made World war profits of a mere $250,000,000, or, according to Senator Nye, a return of 400 per cent on the investment. Verily, the stream of blood which flows from the battlefields of the world becomes a stream of molten gold pouring into the coffers of Dupont, Vickers, and Schneider-Creusot.

Greedy in their gold-grabbing, the arms-makers realize that more wars mean more profits; and the second charge against them is that they foment war scares and stir up strife and hatred between nations. In the recent Sino-Japanese fight over Manchuria, when the League of Nations was bending every effort to make peace, Schneider and Skoda got control of Shanghai newspapers and used them to shriek for war. It was this same Skoda concern which financed Hitler so he could buy arms, thus scaring away from Europe an already timid dove of peace.

Since, then, the profit motive makes for more wars, it is only common sense to remove the profits from war.

Able men urge two measures to strike at one of the greatest causes of war—the profit motive. A measure is pending before Congress by which all industry would be conscripted when this country is at war, to prevent profiteering. I do not wish now to discuss the merits of universal conscription, but I do urge war time control over the armaments industry. The great captains of industry would thereby receive the pay of army officers. The second part of the plan has been urged upon Congress by Presidents Coolidge and Roosevelt. It calls for an international treaty providing for a universal embargo on arms shipments to warring countries. It is plain that such reduction of income would not only kill the big gun mans' desire to see this country at war, but would make him outdo Bryan in championing peace. As for foreign wars, what would be a higher crime in the munitions world, than stirring up war in countries to which immediately all arms shipments must stop?

Let us see how this plan meets other evils of the situation. The third charge against the arms-makers is that they violate international treaties. For instance, they violated the Brussels Act of 1890, which prevented shipping arms into Africa. This gun-running traffic armed the slave raiders who devastated the Soudan. The China Arms Embargo of 1919-1929 being violated, the ravages of internal war swept over this unhappy country already plagued by bandits, hunger, and violent death. Why, you ask, have these agreements failed? Because they were not universal. Because it was unfair to expect the powers who signed them, not to sell arms, when less idealistic countries were reaping bloody profits. The Coolidge-Roosevelt embargo is designed to prevent *all* nations from selling. Universal agreement has successfully controlled the narcotics trade. The arms trade would be even easier to control, for one can hardly imagine the smuggling of an anti-aircraft gun in a loaf of bread—of ordinary size, at least.

The fourth charge against these dealers of death is that they get neutral nations into trouble with warring nations by shipping arms to one or both of the belligerents. Our doughboys charged into the fiery hell of war shouting, "Remember the Lusitania!" The sinking of the Lusitania, carrying ammunition, was one of the main events which drew the United States into the World war, for which the next generation will still be paying. Under the embargo no arms could be shipped, and there would not be that constant sore spot in the eyes of the warring nation whose enemy was getting arms.

The fifth charge against the arms-makers is that they needlessly prolong wars by arming both sides, and often make peace efforts utterly useless. The fight between Bolivia and Paraguay was prolonged only because of arms imports. In many instances they make bloodshed possible where it would be actually impossible without a foreign arms supply. For example, in Cuba an American agent urged the Machado government to buy arms for protection against the Mendieta faction, while he was urging the Mendieta group to buy machine guns and bombs to overthrow the Machado government. It is plain that stopping arms shipments would shorten wars, and would often make warfare comparatively bloodless or even impossible. You may fear that nations could store up sufficient arms to wage a long war. Yet early in the World war, France and England, two of the world's five greatest *producers* of arms, had to buy from our arms-makers, with money borrowed from the United States. Now, who will repay our government? Who will pay the war debt except the American people?

The sixth, and by far the most shocking charge against the arms merchants, is that they actively oppose peace measures. It is known that Schneider controlled the leading newspapers in Paris which defended Japan's land-grabbing attempts in Manchuria and fought the League's attempts to settle the dispute. With an embargo in effect, Japan could not have bought from Schneider even her normal, peace-time arms supply. Schneider would have been tearing his hair to see peace restored. In this country we find that in 1932, when the Fish resolution, providing for a world-wide embargo on arms, was brought up in Congress, one Dupont official wrote another that he had got in touch with General McFarland, Admiral Latimer, and Captain Cage, and he said: "Captain Cage will . . have the (embargo) bill opposed in the House." The bill failed. Under the proposed plan, there would already be a world-wide embargo on arms sales, and there would thus be no need for the death traffickers to exert their evil influence in Congress, and in the War and Navy Departments.

The arms-makers stand indicted and convicted before the high court of public opinion on six charges. Profiteering, fomenting war, violating treaties, embarrassing neutral nations in war times, prolonging or even making war possible, and fighting peace; these are their offenses inspired by their lust for profits and ever more profits. Let us conscript the arms industry, limit incomes in war times, and thwart profiteering. Let us work for a world-wide embargo on arms. All great movements have had small beginnings; and the influence of those who believe in the measures will be felt in ever-widening circles, and some day bear fruit in humanitarian legislation which will kill the profit motive. Unless we do destroy the profit motive, war will be hastened in its coming by those parasites who sit around a dividend table, far removed from the fields of fire and flame where their devilish machines hurtle human souls into eternity, and there in some back room count their cash, every dollar of which was wrung from a human life.

COLLECTIVE SECURITY [6]

The consequence to our country of carrying this policy (of parallel action) thru to its logical conclusion is to involve us unnecessarily in the wars both of Asia and of Europe.

A realistic analysis of the present state of the world shows the so-called "collective security" system to have broken down, certainly temporarily. It broke down first in Manchuria, then in Ethiopia and again in China. Modern war has become a suicidal adventure between great powers and no government has the right to plunge its people into an unnecessary war. The theory that, in this heavily armed world, nations will risk war, perhaps on the other side of the world, when their vital interests are not involved and solely out of altruism, is untenable. This theory of peace was contingent in President Wilson's mind upon universal disarmament as pledged in the Covenant of the League and in the Versailles Treaty, a pledge that was broken by nations that are now calling other nations "treaty-breakers." The theory was contingent also on a League of Nations with adequate provision for peaceful change when conditions in a changing world become unjust and intolerable to any of the parties concerned. The iniquitous Versailles Treaty and the failure of the World War victors to give substance to Article 19 of the League Covenant combined with other factors into which we do not need to enter here to wreck for the present the great hope of world organization for peace to which President Wilson gave birth.

In place of this collective system, we see now two blocs of three nations each, loosely bound together by ties of common interest, pitted against each other. One bloc is popularly called the "democracies." A more accurate definition of it would be the "imperialist-commun-

[6] From testimony of Frederick J. Libby, National Council for the Prevention of War, before the House Committee on Naval Affairs, February 10, 1938.

ist" group, since it is composed of the British Empire, ruling over one-fourth of the world; the French Empire, which includes most of North Africa and a considerable slice of China and has a population of 100 million making it the second largest empire in the world; and Soviet Russia, whose 160 million people occupy one-sixth of the earth's habitable area.   Over against this bloc is the fascist or "anti-communist" bloc, comprising Germany, Italy and Japan, sometimes called the "treaty-breaking, aggressor nations."   They are realtively poor nations and are likely to become the spokesmen for many others as against the rich or "peace-loving" nations, as we like to call ourselves.   There is, however, a reason for our loving peace that is less praiseworthy than the term indicates.

As between these two blocs of powers most of the other nations of the world are trying to remain neutral. Norway and Sweden, which have not been in war for more than a hundred years; Denmark and Holland, which stayed out of the World war for four and one-half years, altho it was in their backyard; Switzerland, and now Belgium and Poland, typify the European nations that see no reason why they should involve themselves in a war not of their own making and which they find themselves powerless to prevent.   The Canadian Minister to this country, Sir Herbert Marler, was quoted by the *New York Herald-Tribune* of October 27, 1937, as saying to the Canadian Club of New York at a dinner given in his honor: "I do not claim that we will be able to prevent war; we do intend to do all in our power to avoid war."   Secretary Cordell Hull took a similar attitude toward wars arising in other continents in his superb manifestation of statesmanship at the Pan-American Conference at Buenos Aires.   The words which he repeatedly used and which express unquestionably the fixed determination of the great majority of our people and of people everywhere were these: "We must create on this hemisphere an area of peace and sanity in a war-mad world." While he did not succeed in getting unanimous agreement because of the opposition particularly of Argentina to a clear-cut neutrality policy in the case of a European war, he did secure a treaty under which any signatory may initiate consultation with the other American states regarding our several neutrality policies when war threatens non-American nations.

Such being the world we now live in as it appears to some of us, the supreme question in our foreign policy is whether or not we shall accept the invitation extended to us by the British Empire under many attractive slogans to defend, by war if necessary, its great interests in Asia, while it is itself fully occupied in Europe. That we should have to fight alone against Japan if our bluff is called seems clear from conditions in Europe. The sinking of a British ship or two in the Mediterranean by "pirates" would suffice to prevent the departure of any substantial portion of the British fleet for Asiatic waters. The cost of a war with Japan, so a member of the President's Cabinet told me just preceding the last London naval conference, would be forty billion dollars. Higher estimates are heard today. Admiral Leahy has been quoted here as saying that our fleet would need to be at least three times the size of Japan's. But in addition to the fleet and to the airplanes a huge armada of transports would be required to make the attempt to land troops with full equipment, ammunition and supplies on the coast of Japan against the resistance of Japan's army and airforce, and in sufficient strength to escape annihilation before reinforcements arrived. I understand that there is grave doubt in army circles if this military operation is humanly possible. The latest failure of such an attempt was the ghastly massacre of the Australian and New Zealand troops at Gallipoli.

Since we should count the cost, and the full cost, of the proposed course of action before embarking on it, let us suppose for the sake of argument that we succeeded in defeating Japan after a long and bloody war. It is safe to say that we should not want under any circumstances to annex Japan nor permanently to occupy it. Nor are we likely to want to occupy or annex China and its problems. We have abandoned imperialism and are, I trust, about to set free the Philippines in fulfilment of our pledge. So our troops would eventually be permitted to return home to their native shore. Then what would happen in Japan and China? Would not China in her vast poverty, and perhaps Japan, probably go communist? Would not Russia, by propaganda and without the necessity of conquest, readily bring all of eastern Asia at least into the communist regime and within her own sphere of influence? Thus by their death our boys would have made one-third of the world communist—*not* democratic.

Our country, on the other hand, in a world-wide depression that would follow the next major war, would be likely to remain under the military dictatorship that had fought the war, and to do so willingly, as a preferable alternative to chaos and communism. Thus the net result of the untold sacrifice and misery that our country would have undergone to fight this war would be to turn Asia red, while we lost our democracy in fascism.

It is a common practice for military and naval men to propound hypothetical questions as to what would happen if Germany and Italy, for example, were to forget all their ambitions in Europe and Africa and launch a joint attack, presumably with money borrowed from Britain, France or ourselves, upon Brazil. To me the dangers inherent in the President's proposal of "concerted effort" in the Far East are far more real and immediate than these imagined conditions. I regard the supernavy and the passage in peace-time of the mobilization plan as the kind of "day-by-day decisions" which bring us nearer a fatal war.

But suppose we do not join in concerted action against the so-called aggressor nations. What is the alternative constructive policy? Anne O'Hare McCormick, in a dispatch from London to the *New York Times* a few weeks ago, wrote in substance as follows: The British are watching American public opinion as never before. If the Americans will fight, Britain will stiffen her attitude toward Germany and will not have to make concessions. If America will not fight, concessions will be necessary.

It is my conviction that the just grievances of Germany must be met if war is to be avoided. The British have never published the terms offered by Hitler to Lord Halifax and the suspicion is inevitable that they were reasonable. The only alternative to war is peaceful change and we must make adequate provisions for the meeting of just grievances if war is to be averted. World disarmament and ultimate peace hinge on the progressive removal of the causes of war.

WAR OR PEACE [7]

Are was as a nation in danger? To the north we have a peaceable and friendly neighbor whose people have a common interest with ours. To the south we have a neighbor which if permitted to work out its own problems has no thought of warfare. If the Hearsts and the Standard Oil companies of this country seek investment in Mexico let them do so at their own risk, and let them abide by the Constitution and laws of Mexico. (Several years ago a small company was formed in my home town and invested several thousand dollars in Mexican land. Later we found that the Constitution of Mexico did not permit foreigners to secure title to

[7] From radio address of Knute Hill, Representative from Washington. April 12, 1938. *Congressional Record.* 83:7230. April 18, 1938.

land in Mexico. We took our medicine and did not call on United States troops to punish Mexico.) To the east we have the broad Atlantic across which it would be a foolhardy attempt for a Mussolini or a Hitler to transport an army capable of conquering the most powerful country in the world. Moreover, those dictators have and will have their hands full in Europe. To the west is the expansive Pacific. It is ridiculous to even suggest that there is any danger from a Japanese invasion. Japan insists on Asia for the Asiatics. Is that anything else but an oriental Monroe Doctrine? Again, Japan is having her hands full with an embattled and determined China which considers herself a considerable part of the Asiatics. Furthermore, the people of Japan will not remain docile if the war lords seek conquest across the Pacific.

What is adequate defense? We all want adequate defense. Such men as Admiral Sims and Generals Rivers and Hagood state in unmistakable language that our present naval defense is adequate. Admiral William S. Sims, commander of the American Fleet in European waters during the World war, has stated that the United States is safe from attack because—and I quote:

No foreign power or group of powers can operate across the oceans and stand a chance in combat with the American navy and planes operating from home bases.

Gen. William C. Rivers has written:

Neither Japan nor America has enough merchant ships for fleet auxiliaries should there be a desire to send an armada across 6,500 miles of sea. We have 488 merchant vessels in foreign trade. The fleet alone would need 900 such ships—to transport an army, there would be required some 2,500 additional merchant ships. The Panama Canal is more than 9,000 miles from Japan and 2,000 miles directly south of New York. The passage of an armada to the canal across such a vast area as the mid-Pacific would be an adventure so fraught with difficulties as to be impracticable.

We are assembling in the North Pacific Ocean what I believe is the greatest aggregation of fighting ships and combat airplanes the world has ever seen in one spot. I feel that by no use of the imagination can one correctly say that our battle assemblage in the North Pacific Ocean is required for the defense of Alaska, the Hawaiians, the continental United States, and the Panama Canal, our normal line of defense in the event of a war. The only method of using such a battle armada as we retain in the North Pacific Ocean against any other power in the Pacific is by applying the illusory and dangerous doctrine of some extremists—that an aggressive offense is always the best defense. Such a doctrine may well at times evoke a war thru the provocation of such armament.

General Johnson Hagood wrote:

But no such force (able to inflict damage) could come across the Atlantic Ocean, because there is no nation that has a sufficient army and at the same time a sufficient number of ships and a navy to support it.

And lastly, listen to Gen. Smedley Butler, the "fighting marine," who says that any invading nation would have to bring over 1,000,000 men and use 7,500,000 tons of ocean-going craft to transport supplies, where the whole ocean-going merchant fleet of all the nations of the world is not that much, according to his figures.

Let us have aircraft, anti-aircraft, mines, submarines, and light cruisers instead of hulks of battleships which cost $80,000,000 and can be used mostly in foreign waters where $200,000 enemy bombers can sink then in five minutes.

Some men, even Senator Borah, insist on the freedom of the seas. That is our right, but how foolhardy to insist on it when the nations traversing the seven seas are at war and all the international laws and treaties are scraps of paper. I have an inalienable right as a citizen to walk down the public street. But when warring factions are killing each other on that street, it is the part of prudence and wisdom for me to refrain from insisting on my right.

When and if the world becomes sane again, then the responsible nations may organize an international police force to capture, and an international tribunal to punish international outlaws the same as our G-men and Federal courts punish kidnappers. Until we have a real world peace conference at which a weary world can then plan for lasting peace, our United States had better stay out.

BRIEF EXCERPTS

I charge that this tremendous expenditure is not for collective security or adequate defense as the President has said.

It is the first step toward an Anglo-American alliance in which, thru joint naval action, the battle fleets of America and Great Britain, in the ratio of fifteen of ours to six of theirs, will attempt to roll up the Japanese navy. *Norman Thomas. New York Times. Ja. 29, '38. p. 4.*

We can prepare in one of two ways: either by building up our army and navy to the greatest extent possible, and going our lone way as before; or by joining in with other law abiding states to maintain respect for law and order in the community of nations. Obviously the latter is the cheapest and safest way; I hope that it will not require another World war to teach the American people that lesson. *Clyde Eagleton. Womans Press. Mr. '38. p. 159.*

Sir Edward Grey, England's great minister for foreign affairs, declared that he could have prevented the outbreak of war if he could have gotten the diplomats of the opposing nations together around a table. I would make very sure that such a table is at hand should another crisis arise, and that the nations are accustomed to sitting around it in a friendly discussion of their common problems. *C. S. Potts. Southwestern Social Science Quarterly. S. '35. p. 10.*

The Admirals are agreed that we cannot worst the Japanese navy in Japanese waters. Then let us stop irritating Japan by maneuvers almost under her nose. If they must be held in the Pacific, let them be east of Hawaii and let us stop building airdromes and forts where no one can look upon them as anything except as threats to Japan. Considering Germany's activity in Venezuela (1902), Santo Domingo (1903), and Haiti (1910-12, 1914), what would the United States have thought, had she announced that the maneuvers of her fleet would be held in the Caribbean in 1914? *David Y. Thomas. South Atlantic Quarterly. Ap. '37. p. 133-4.*

If our generation knew a hundredth part as much about the mechanism of wise government as every boy knows about Buicks and Fords, the world would not be in peril of another war, and the safest nation in the world would not demand now, for the first time, that it have as great a navy as any upon earth.

When the nations are organized as adequately as are our cities, the World Court, like the Supreme Court at Washington, will require no other or more force behind it than that of public opinion. *Lucia Ames Mead. Homiletic Review. May. '34. p. 349, 350.*

To understand the significance of armaments they must be viewed in their totality. They will then be seen to constitute an enormous war-machine dominating the life of nations, and driving it in the direction of war; the parts so interrelated that when one starts into action the whole begins to move. Nothing could be more absurd than to suppose that the totality of the world's armaments can be so manipulated, by treaties or diplomatic arts, as to suppress its own activities as a war-making instrument and convert it into an instrument for keeping the peace. *L. P. Jacks. Co-operation or Coercion. p. 84-5. E. P. Dutton & Co. N.Y. '38.*

If a genuine collective peace system is being tried and a certain measure of offensive rearmament is necessary to keep it preponderant, the public must attach conditions to such rearmament. These are: that there shall be no menacing armaments except those that are definitely limited and coordinated for collective security; no provocation except sanctions against any aggressor; no commitments except the Covenant of the League and a Europe-wide system of collective security against aggression from the air. *Jonathan Griffin. Alternative to Rearmament. p.* 212. *Macmillan & Co. Lond.* '36.

No sane man believes that an arms race ends in peace. But all sane men know that one-sided armaments lead to war. Whoever or whatever is responsible for this world-at-arms that now confronts us—and an examination of conscience on that bitter and debatable question leaves no power blameless—the tragic fact emerges that if we are to revert to the old balance-of-power system as the alternative to a system of collective security, peaceful change and shared responsibility, then we must also revert to a balance of forces, including military forces. *Editorial. New York Times. Ap.* 27, '37. *p.* 22.

What will be the end of this mad race in armament? Unless a halt is called it will lead to war, resulting in revolution, fascism, communism, death and destruction of a large part of civilization. The staggering sums now being spent on armaments by Great Britain, France, Germany, Russia, Italy, Japan, China, United States and other nations are a harsh reminder of the fact that we are living in a militarized world in which nations are unwilling to put their trust in the pacts and treaties they have signed. Force to the uttermost appears to be the present slogan. *World Alliance for International Friendship Through the Churches. News Letter. Ja.* '38. *p.* 4.

The great stumbling block to the efforts for international peace which have from time to time been made
has proved to be the military establishments maintained
by all the prosperous states. These are today the great
menace to world peace. They are vast organizations
which tend to develop a sort of corporate soul. They
seek to grow and to justify their existence and even while
prating about serving only for defense they provoke
jealousy, suspicion and emulation. Moreover, besides
stimulating the creating of similar machines in other
nations they keep alive the prestige and glory of the
soldier's career and serve as a perpetual reminder and
example of mistrust, hostility and brute force. *Robert R.
Logan. Herald of the Star. N. '27.*

The world can have peace whenever the world wants
it enough to fulfill this condition. The major precondi-
tion of war, that makes it almost inevitable, is sixty-odd
national states refusing to surrender to a central court
and administration one item of their sovereignty.

Some day the consummation will come—concerning
which our children's children will think us imbecile because we did not achieve it—a central court, a central
administration, controlling whatever force is necessary
for international government in the form of international
police, and the different nationalities will have surrendered
not all their sovereignty, but this one useless and disastrous item in it, their right to the exercise of violence.
*Harry Emerson Fosdick. Reviews of Reviews. My. '37.
p. 55.*

We know today that in 1908 neither the British nor
the German government was planning to attack the other.
We know that in June 1914 neither the French nor the
German nor the Russian government desired or worked
for war; that they were all in great measure victims of

"a fearful misunderstanding"; that they "stumbled and staggered" into war because they and their peoples had all come to think that war was "inevitable"—inevitable, since their "enemies" were determined to force it on. And we know today where many of the "spy-scares" came from, how the "fears of invasion" were created, how "intentions" were twisted and "motives slandered," how the idea was "falsely spread" that other nations "violently desired war." *Philip Noel-Baker. The Private Manufacture of Armaments. Oxford Univ. Press. N.Y. '37. p. 555.*

We are told today that great navies insure peace. Is that the story of the Armada? Spain built a great navy for the purpose of making Spain the master of the seas, and of bringing complete control and security to Spain. What was the result. It brought war and defeat and ruin.

Was peace insured as the result of the building of a great navy by Germany? Germany set out to build a navy which would insure her control of a vast portion of the European countries and make her safe in her enterprises. She had security by land in her army; she desired security and mastery by sea. Within 20 years she had suffered complete collapse from her enterprise. War came and we all know the result. *Sen. William E. Borah. Congressional Record. My. 2, '38. p. 8010.*

Battleships of the kind that Mr. Davis wants the United States to build have little to do with peace, less with defense, and nothing at all with democracy. To match Britain's rearmament program means to risk war in Asia and the Pacific while Britain is busy elsewhere. The purpose of such a war, furthermore, has no bearing whatever upon the defense of the territorial United States. The size of the battleships Mr. Davis wants to

build leave no doubt on that score. Finally, whatever the
aims of the United States may be, it cannot fight a foreign war without establishing a military dictatorship.
Even the most innocent believer in sanctions and collective security can hardly doubt that their application will
mean the end of democracy in the United States, no
matter what happens elsewhere. *Quincy Howe. England Expects Every American to Do His Duty. Simon
& Schuster. N.Y. '37. p. 209.*

The war machinery of the world, held in separate
nations' hands, mounting in quantity and in deadliness,
has increased the danger rather than diminished it. It is
as tho a mining camp, becoming at last impatient of its
frequent murders, decided to end them. So each miner
buys himself two automatic pistols instead of his one old
shooting-iron. And then, finding that these have not accomplished the desired result,—for there are more kill-
ings than ever,—bethink them, each, to add to the two
automatics a machine gun apiece and a capped stick of
dynamite for use against the neighbor's house,—"insurance against trouble," they say, as they carry these goods
home. *George M. Stratton. Problems of War and
Peace in the Society of Nations. Univ. of California
Press. '37. p. 153.*

If we are going to have a civilized world, we must
have a potentially effective police force. No city, no
state, no nation can exist without police, without the sanction, behind the law, of ultimate force to be exercised on
behalf of the community as a whole. And the use of
international police power is fundamentally different
from war. War, in the sense of the use of armed force
by one nation to impose its will on another, never is justified. The exercise of armed force as a police measure
to insure the safety of the members of the international

community and to maintain that collective security which must be achieved if civilization is to survive, is justified when circumstances make it necessary. Moreover, the existence of that ultimate sanction of force, to be exercised on behalf of the community of nations as a whole, is essential. *Grover Clark. Contacts Between the East and West. Institute of Public Affairs, Univ. of Va. Jl. 16, '37. p. 7.*

The belief that British armaments are a guarantee of peace, tho apparently sincerely held by British admirals, air-marshals, and cabinet ministers responsible for the services, is not shared by Germans, Italians, or Japanese· it is not held by Frenchmen or Spaniards or Belgians, unless there is also a pretty solid guarantee that the armaments are going to be used on their side in the next war. This policy, therefore, increases the armaments race and the international uncertainty and instability. That is a situation in which, sooner or later, some dictator will inevitably be impelled to gamble with war or a threat of war, and then the guns will go off. Whether we are in the war or out of it will be determined by chance or even panic, not by our own considered decision. *Leonard Woolf. Political Quarterly (Lond.) Ja.-Mr. '37. p. 26-7.*

More serious than the financial aspects of this policy are its implications for world politics and the nation's hope of peace. The naval policy which the Roosevelt administration is thus about to fasten on the country involves, it is clear, a navy overwhelmingly larger than any other nation possesses. To do the things which this declaration of policy says must be done, the American navy must be able to whip not only any other navy but any other combination of navies wherever our commerce or our citizens happen to be. Which is to say, anywhere in the world. It is perfectly safe to predict that no such naval policy can be adopted without sending a thrill of fear thru every other maritime nation, and no building program designed to implement such a policy can be entered upon without precipitating the most suicidal naval building race ever known. *Christian Century. F. 23, '38. p. 231.*

By still refusing to join actively in the efforts to get the machinery of international relations really organized and working effectively, we Americans have told the other nations in the clearest possible way that we still adhere to the old idea that every nation must look to its own armed might for protection and that we think collective security is not much more than a pleasant dream. We still in effect say that the world is a world of gangster nations, among which every nation must carry its own guns.

Since we still so act as to show that this is our attitude, how can we expect Japan, or China, to take any other stand? Or any of the European countries? Because the United States is the richest and potentially most powerful nation, our influence is the greatest—whether that influence be exercised, by our example, negatively on the side of the old system of antagonisms or positively on the side of a civilized world by our actions in cooperating with other nations to establish real collective security. *Grover Clark. Contacts Between The East and West. Institute of Public Affairs, Univ. of Va. Jl. 16, '37. p. 6-7.*

How far should the United States go in reducing armaments?

Just as far as public opinion will permit! Armaments are a source of peril, not a means of security. Permanent peace cannot be assured until huge armies are disbanded and gigantic fleets are dismantled. "No race in armaments can avert war," declares General F. P. Crozier, of the British Army, retired. "The re-

verse is the case. Our slogan 'if you want peace, prepare for war,' is as dead and out-of-date as the dull
military minds—'duds,' we call them—which still hold
to it. It is utter rubbish." The United States should
take the initiative in scrapping the war system for three
primary reasons: our shores are not in danger of invasion by a foreign foe; the use of armed force in
seeking to protect the property and lives of our citizens
in other lands is inadvisable; the securing of public
support for the huge budget of more than seven million
dollars required for the current expenses of the army
and navy each year necessitates preparedness campaigns
which create suspicion, fear and enmity and tend to
perpetuate the military philosophy. *Sherwood Eddy and
Kirby Page. What Shall We Do About War? Eddy
and Page. N.Y. n.d. p.* 63-4.

The most important of the factors which led the
United States into the World war will operate in another war of similar type. If most of the great powers
are involved the government will become convinced that
only by entering can we prevent a peace treaty adversely
affecting our political position in the world. Such an
effect would surely be assumed if the treaty challenged
the Monroe Doctrine thru a transfer of Caribbean Islands, or established a single dominant military power
in Europe or Asia. Furthermore, unless the government
imposed a wholly unlikely censorship on the press and
other means of communication, unneutral sentiments
would develop, incidents injurious to the United States
would occur, the "dance of death" would become attractive, diplomatic controversies would prove futile, opinion
would become war-minded and dominantly on one
side or the other. Isolation cannot be sufficiently thoro-
going to keep a great power like the United States out
of a general European war which lasts for any

considerable length of time. We can well afford to risk participation in a cooperative program carrying even a faint promise of preventing such a war or stopping it in its early stages. *Quincy Wright. Southern Review. Ap. '38. p. 761.*

In answer to the contention that the use of force will only serve to widen the area of war, the proponents of international machinery for the maintenance of peace declare that the very contrary is the case; that if, in a given case, a nation knows that it will have turned against it the major force of mankind, it will hesitate long before taking up arms. A firm determination to put down aggression will narrow, not extend, the sphere of war. As for the difficulty of determining the aggressor, it is not impossible to set up tests which, if not mathematically accurate, will at least operate in the majority of cases. The Covenant itself sets up one such test in declaring that a nation which refuses to submit its dispute to arbitration or conciliation must be regarded as having violated its obligations, and hence as exposed to economic and military measures of a punitive character. It is within the province of statesmanship to evolve tests still more inclusive and satisfactory. The task can be solved, if it is faced. If there is a common will to maintain peace, the mechanism to translate this will into action will be evolved. *Dexter Perkins. World Unity. My. '30. p. 127.*

The American people are confronted by a decision of the highest importance. If we continue our attempt to equal the British fleet at a time when, for purely European reasons, that fleet is to be increased by 65 per cent at once and presumably much more in the future, we shall have entered on a course that can only lead eventually to national bankruptcy and to war. The alternative is for us to prepare a military establishment in terms of our own necessities and in the light of the fact that we have renounced any effort to build a world-wide empire. In making this decision, traditional habits of thought, traditional institutions are of no use to us. The militarist who says that because we have always had a navy we must now have a grotesquely inflated one is not being, as he imagines, a conservative. On the contrary he would have us embark on a radical and reckless experiment. The questions we must answer are: Do we intend to live at peace and mind our own business? If so, what sort of military system, and of what size, is best calculated to implement that policy? *New Republic. Mr. 3, '37. p. 98.*

Society's responsibility for peace brings us directly to the problem of a new federalization of nations, by means of which we might not only outlaw war, but perhaps eliminate war and aggressor thru the sharing of common interests in a world-wide Union of Nations.

To this end our educational system, our press, our politics, our business attitudes, and the spirit of our home life should be in complete harmony. Instead of glorifying war and its traditions, the whole world should actually outlaw it in every aspect of life. The people of several nations even now are being led astray by leaders moved by grandiose ambitions, or by those who would be profiteers of war, and this should not be. Instead of allowing an entire nation to become involved in war simply to protect a few venturesome persons or the foreign invested interests of a few industrialists, let it be understod that they are subject to their own risk in foreign countries. When false leadership, imperialism, and exploitation by a privileged few can no longer hide behind the flag and national loyalty, there will be removed what is probably the most important barrier to international goodwill, and the formation of a superworld state, with peace for all nations, will be that much nearer fulfillment. *John Eric Nordskog. Sociology and Social Research. Ja.-F. '38. p. 244-5.*

Pope Pius XI has placed his discerning finger upon the two great provocatives of war: armament and exaggerated nationalism. In his letter on "Unemployment," His Holiness declares: "The unbridled race for armaments is on the one hand the effect of the rivalry among nations and on the other the cause of the withdrawal of enormous sums from the public wealth and hence not the smallest of contributions to the present extraordinary crisis."

The whole history of humanity shows the folly of seeking to find security and lasting peace by outstripping other nations in the race for superior armaments. The very effort engenders fear, suspicion, antagonism. Reliance comes to be placed not on justice or right, but on might. In this atmosphere of suspicion and tension a tiny spark ignites the tinder box which sets the world aflame. When the war spirit breaks loose, reason and conscience are ruthlessly trampled under foot. Codes of ethics are consigned to the scrap heap. All become obsessed with the single passion—to maim, to kill, and to slaughter the greatest number of human beings. Such is the vicious circle to which the race for competitive armament has always led. Such too is the tragic denoument in which it has inevitably ended—the catastrophe of war. *Rev. John A. O'Brien. The Church and Disarmament. p. 7-9.*

There is a seeming contradiction between the conscious individual aversion to war and the collective preparedness to wage war. Civilized twentieth century man still possesses strong, fierce and destructive instincts, which have not been sublimated, or only partly so, and which break loose as soon as the community to which he belongs feels itself threatened by danger. It should be realized that the fighting-instinct, if well directed, gives energy for much that is good and beautiful. But the same instinct may create chaos if it breaks loose from all restraint, making use of the greatest discoveries of the human intellect.

The apathy with regard to the actions and intrigues of the international traffic in arms is surprising to anyone who realizes the dangers into which this traffic threatens to lead them. It should be realized that it is foolish to suffer certain groups of persons to derive personal profit from the death of millions of men.

We come to you with the urgent advice to arouse the nations to the realization of fact and the sense of collective self-preservation, these powerful instincts being the strongest allies for the elimination of war.

The heightening of the moral and religious sense in your people tends to the same end. *From Open Letter of the Netherlands Medical Association to Statesmen Throughout the World. Church Peace Union. News Letter. Ap.* 30, '36. *p.* 4-5.

Nothing in these huge expenditures is more shocking than the estimated cost of battleships. The two provided for by the bill just passed by the House are estimated to cost $71,000,000 each. What the battleships authorized by the supplemental program will cost, no naval authorities will even guess. This is an appalling upward leap in the price of what the navy calls its "battle wagons." When the two capital ships now building were authorized, their cost was estimated at about $50,000,000. They will actually cost in excess of $60,000,000. When the two approved last week were first proposed, their price was set at $60,000,000. But the appropriation now being jammed thru sets their cost at more than $70,000,000. That means a $20,000,000 jump in the cost of battleships in three years! And it must be remembered that after this cost is paid, another ten to fifteen million is required to place each ship in commission. Costs of other naval vessels are going up in proportion. Destroyers that were built for $1,000,000 at the time of the war are now costing the government $5,000,000. And they talk about taking the profits out of war! *Christian Century. F. 2, '38. p. 132.*

I thoroly believe that our legal rights should be maintained, if necessary by the use of force. The question then is: what force should be used? You may, indeed you must, choose between our own unaided national force and the collective force of the organized society of nations. If you reject the latter and choose the former, then it is your duty, I think, to work for the strongest possible army and navy. But this, of course, is exactly the rule of anarchy and the rule of might over right which we are seeking to abolish. To my mind, the only possible way by which the functions that have so long been served by war can be otherwise served, is by an international organization which can impartially settle disputes, cooperatively remedy wrongs, and collectively enforce rights. Such an organization must have force behind it, because the only way to meet the criminal state which employs force is by a superior force. Our share in the collective enterprise would be smaller than the cost of independent action of our own; the result would be more just; the risk would be less. There are some who say that such military sanctions are war, and that, therefore, we would not have abolished war. Surely such collective military action would be regarded as police work, rather than as war; but whatever it is, it is necessary. You cannot have peace merely by talking about it, or by hating war, or by writing words on paper; you have to pay a price, and sometimes a heavy price, to get it. *Clyde Eagleton. Institute of Public Affairs. Proceedings, 1936. p. 164.*

One hundred and twenty or more million Americans want no more of war. These same people, however, will willingly give their all in defense of their country if it is attacked. They fairly assume that such an event is not at all likely. They wonder who might be so foolish as to even dream of attacking us. Then they quite naturally wonder why we are now annually spending three times as much for national defense as we were spending prior to our entry in the war to end war. They note, too, that while the burden of preparing for war is increasingly difficult to bear, those who today cry about the inadequacy of our national defense are the same as bemoaned the inadequacy of our defense of 1915 and 1916. One day there will be general awakening of people to the fact that these mad programs of preparing for war pay large profits to some few people and industries and that this prospect of profit plays no small part in driving a world to such madness as we find now in preparing for more war. When enough people do thus awaken there is certain to be such a public demand as will cause governments to slow their pace and move in a direction to discourage or destroy the prospect of profit from war itself and from preparation for war. *Senator Gerald P. Nye. Address. World Peaceways. N.Y. O. 3, '37.*

The danger of an attack on our shores by an evil aggressor nation is relatively remote. But again let us suppose the alarmists of the administration are right. It would still be doubtful wisdom to put the sum asked for by Mr. Roosevelt into new warships to the neglect of essential social services. There are a hundred theories of what makes a nation great in war, but all of them include national morale. There is no intention here to dig up the question of what unloosed the World war, but one factor unquestionably was the knowledge among the German military chiefs that a revolt against English rule had broken out among Irish tenant farmers, and that the Russian economic system was reeling under the tyranny and incompetence of the Tsars. The same domestic problems about which the voters of this country are alarmed, bad health, slum housing, rural poverty, lack of educational facilities, all constitute military weakness. A nation with the miraculous industrial technique of the United States can, in time of crisis, turn out airplane engines, plate armor, tanks, submachine guns at will, but without healthy, educated, loyal citizens cannot call itself a virile country, and cannot win wars. To conserve natural resources, health and morale is the first business of a program of defense, whether against internal scourges or foreign enemies. *New Republic. Mr. 30, '38. p. 236.*

The agencies for international understanding are really serving the cause of moral disarmament. The two ideals are substantially the same. A mere mention of the efforts that are directly and indirectly striving for peace and understanding among the peoples of the world shows the magnitude of their reach and scope.

The problem confronting the present generation is difficult but not insoluble. In the last analysis it amounts to the discovery of the proper balance to be established between the armament claims assertible by the nations for legitimate defense purposes and the aspirations of the great majorities of human beings who want peace and normalcy with a chance to rear and educate their children undisturbed by the grim presence of Mars who as has been well said, determines "not who is right but who is left." It is the thesis of the speaker that genuine moral disarmament and world understanding will solve the problem of material armament including the special problem of arms traffic for private profit. There is no panacea for peace. It is necessary for true friends of world peace and recovery to play upon all the fiddle strings, not upon one only. We must gradually and progressively build up international faith and confidence in the institutions for peaceful settlement such as the League of Nations, the World Court, the Pan-American Union, et cetera. We must strive for moral disarmament, and we must control the profits of munitions makers who would cash in upon the sufferings and agonies of millions of their fellows thru modern mechanical and chemical warfare. *J. Eugene Harley. Institute of International Affairs. Proceedings,* 1934. *p.* 190, 200-1.

The menace to British and American democracy comes, not from Germany or Italy or Japan, but from forces within their own borders. The economic systems in these countries break down. Millions are thrown out of work. The states manage to float on borrowed funds. Politicians and business leaders stand in bewilderment in the presence of the phenomenon. The maladjustment in the moving parts of our economic systems seems to have arrived at the crisis stage. And when an economic system breaks down it is natural to look for apostles of new philosophies, to press for new economic systems. In all these countries we see communistic and fascist groups contend for power. That struggle has reached a critical juncture in France. It will grow to greater intensity in Britain. It may come here. If it does it is entirely probable that the fascist groups will be more powerful than the left-wing groups. And thus, if our democracy fails to make our economic systems function, our democracies will break down and the fascist groups will assume power.

But this danger threatens us not from the armies of fascist states meditating invasion to impose fascism on us, but from forces and groups within our own borders. If we wish to fight fascism, therefore, it is important for us to recognize where the enemy lies. The way to defend our democracy is to make it work inside our own frontiers. There is but one way to do that and that is to fabricate mechanisms which will make our economic system operate more smoothly. Anything that tends to take our minds off that supremely important task only tends to expose us the more to the real enemy. *John T. Flynn. Asia. Ap. '38. p. 231.*

If bankruptcy and/or war do not result from this mad race, then all precedents will fail. Meanwhile the costs, staggering as they are, are not the worst feature of this mad militarism. Everywhere the armies are becoming so powerful as literally to control the fate of nations. In Russia, if the Red Army decides to unhorse Stalin, he will go. Hitler will rule just as long as he holds the loyalty of his army. The horrible tragedy of Spain shows what can happen when the army turns traitor to the legally constituted government. In Japan the army seems about to have its way with country and people. Nearer home, the dictators in the Caribbean are intrenching themselves by making their armies more efficient. But they can be ousted on the day their troops decide that they want some other "leader" to rule them. So we have the astounding anomaly that the armies which were built up to safeguard countries from external attack have become the chief danger to the states they were to preserve. If it be objected that this has always been the case, I reply that the danger was slight when armies were small professional forces and not "nations in arms." Now that the whole life of nations is being made to center more and more about the military, and that those who control the military are controlling more and more the entire industrial machinery, it will not be surprising if soldiers arrogate to themselves the right to interfere in purely civilian affairs and to prescribe in peace time as well as in war time what form of government their countries shall have. Naturally they nowhere favor democracy. Democracy and militarism cannot mix not even under the Stars and Stripes. *Oswald Garrison Villard. Nation. F. 27, '37. p. 240.*

Belief in armaments as a preventive of war was common in certain circles before 1914, and it seems that some people have not learned any thing on this question since. Every time one nation adds a soldier to its army, or a ship to its navy, others feel that they must add one or two—to maintain peace. And so we are going around in a vicious circle. War preparations by Western powers are countered by war preparations by Japan. Or put it the other way around, if you will. War preparations by Japan are countered by war preparations by Western powers. How long will this unmerry-go-round of war preparation last before there is a crash? The idea that an increase of American armaments or of Japanese armaments will preserve peace is too absurd for discussion.

All this war preparation is for "defense." Defense where? Against whom? In the Pacific and against Japan, says Senator Pittman, Chairman of the Senate Committee on Foreign Relations. Soon after the Spanish-American War Captain Richmond Pearson Hobson raised the "scare" of the Japanese peril and hammered away at it at intervals until his death. He found disciples and now the "scare" has attained much larger proportions under the fostering care of Hobson's followers. In his speech of February 10, 1936, referred to above, Senator Pittman quoted Vice-Adrimal Sankichi Takahashi, commander-in-chief of the Japanese fleet, as saying: "Unless America renounces her naval policy aimed at the expansion and protection of her foreign trade, Japan will be forced to extend her fleet's cruising radius

to New Guinea, Celebes, and Borneo, and establish footholds in Formosa and the mandated South Sea Islands."
And then Senator Pittman added: "He commands, in
language that cannot be misunderstood, that we abandon
our naval policy, refrain from expanding our commerce
in China, and cease the protection of our foreign commerce. . . . Of course Congress will not be bulldozed
into the abandonment of our national defense, the protection of our legitimate foreign trade, our commerce
with China, a friendly nation that is at peace with us
and the rest of the world." *David Y. Thomas. South
Atlantic Quarterly. Ap. '37. p. 124-5.*

There is no direct American interest in any of these
national or international situations as far as their political aspects are concerned. The United States has
no mission to determine, or aid in determining, the kind
of government that any European or Asiatic state shall
have or the relations they shall maintain with their
neighbors. It is not called upon to save the British
Commonwealth from political dismemberment, or to oppose the efforts of Germany or Italy to extend their
political influence in Eastern Europe, the Near East or
the Mediterranean. Only a vivid imagination can see
the likelihood of an attack upon American continental
territory by any European or Asiatic power. It may
very well be concerned, however, over the possibility
of a war which will create something akin to world chaos,
for it would then be called upon to protect American neutral commerce and American citizens and the
property investment of its nationals abroad. It cannot,
in short, remain indifferent to world disorder. It should
have a navy adequate to the protection of its coast and
its seaborne trade, and coast defenses and an army able
to supplement the navy in meeting any sporadic attack.
The danger is that preparedness may go farther than
that. Mr. Roosevelt's Chicago speech, with its sugges-

tion of "quarantining" certain powers whose governments are dictatorships, pointed to the possibility of forcible interference in international controversies, not for the purpose of upholding American rights but with the avowed aim of bringing dictatorships to book. The failure of the Brussels Conference called a halt in that program, if program it was, and it is gratifying to note that the suggestion does not reappear in the naval message which President Roosevelt sent to Congress on Friday. Congress should not fail, however, to scrutinize with the utmost care not only the details of the naval proposals which Mr. Roosevelt has submitted, but also the purposes for which an enlarged navy may be used. It should not be mislead by the plea that naval building will increase employment and stimulate industrial activity, for war expenditures, beyond the legitimate needs of national defense, are unproductive and a navy must be maintained after it is built. *Commercial & Financial Chronicle. Ja. 29, '38. p. 651-2.*

There is a deadly meaning in all these plans and preparations, all these blueprints, all this building and spending. That meaning is war. But what pulls and pressures have been at work here can only be guessed at. Certainly it is not the needs of national defense. The purposes of national defense could be met with one-third the present expenditures. We have been swept up in the European war hysteria. The constant talk of an impending European war has undoubtedly given the American general staffs and American statesmen the military jitters. Much closer home is our fear of a Japanese war—a fear whose flames have been lit and are being persistently fanned by Mr. Hearst's newspaper campaign. To that must be added the pressure exerted here as in every country by the War Department and the general staffs—a pressure that is a compound of bureaucratic pride, professional jealousies, narrowness of world outlook, and the sheer desire to play with toys that you have gone to infinite trouble in making. One of the great dangers in having the whole industrial establishment of the country ready for conscription is that it gives the War Department the sense of security which makes its pressures on Congress and the President all the greater. Add the pressures from professional patrioteers and from the industrialists and lobbyists, whose puppets they are. One of the most active fields for lobbying is the field of war orders. The contracts are fat, the prices are generous, the turnover is great. Here, also, lies the greatest danger, for it is unthinkable that a group of industrialists with War Department contracts already made out would not in a period of industrial stringency feel highly tempted to get the benefit of those contracts. Finally, there is the recurring theme of the use to which an efficient military establishment could be put in any case of civil disturbance. The Japanese phantom is not the only one that our imagination has conjured up; there is also the red-scare phantom. The fact that the army and the National Guard, as the naked power of the state, can be turned against labor struggles is certainly not the least of what recommends the recent army appropriations to those who approve them. *Nation. Ap.* 8, '36. *p.* 436-7.

Everyone says that the navy is to defend us, and and to keep us out of war. But if this is true, then a hideous mistake has apparently been made, lasting over many years. From the testimony of Major General Johnson Hagood, late Commanding General of the Third army and the Eighth Corps Area, and other experts, the inference is plain that the kind of army and navy that we possess is *not* intended to defend this country. If we really wanted to protect our shores, and nothing else, we should do many things that we are not now doing. And we should omit some things in which we are now engaged. Our navy parallels that of Great Britain with almost comical exactness. She is a world-wide empire, whose fleet is intended for worldwide operations. And so is ours.

If we wanted to defend the United States, plus Alaska, Hawaii, the Panama Canal and our Caribbean possessions, what should we do that we are not now doing? In the opinion of these experts, we should spend a substantial sum of money on coast defense, which, in the United States, has been allowed to sink to a scandalously low level. We should devote a great deal of attention to the use of airplanes in conjunction with fixed-gun defense of our principal harbors, many of which are virtually unguarded today. We should supplement these efforts with plans for mine laying and the use of submarines in our coastal waters. We should reduce our fleet to the number and size of vessels necessary to participate in these defensive measures. This would almost certainly mean a reduction in our present number of battleships and big cruisers, types of vessels which are primarily designed to conduct an offensive over long distances. We should in addition have a small and highly mobile mechanized army to fight at home if required. We would need to pay very little attention to transport, since it would be outside our policy to try to carry millions of men across an ocean. We should therefore be able to reduce the vast annual sums that we are now spending in merchant-marine subsidies, and the even vaster sum which the lively Mr. Kennedy proposes to spend. *Bruce Bliven. New Republic. Ja 26, '38. p. 328-9.*

Wherefore preparedness? The answer would be—to avert war—that is, to make war unnecessary!—to enable a country to wage war successfully, whether war be offensive or defensive.

Instead of preparedness averting war and making it unnecessary, instead of preparedness enabling a country to wage war, defensive or offensive, successfully, I hold that preparedness makes war not impossible nor unlikely, but inevitable.

As for claiming that preparedness averts war, I hold that preparedness has never averted war, that is to say, preparedness may postpone a minor or lesser war, only to ensure a major or greater war, and to hasten its coming. Preparedness may be said to avert war only on the presumption that humans and nations would always be at war were it not for the preventive of preparedness. As for preparedness averting war, and the false adage "Si vis pacem para bellum," I cite the most obvious illustration. The European nations were armed to the teeth in 1914. Perefect preparedness did not avert war, the World war, which was brought on not by the shot of a madman at Sarajevo, but made inevitable by the complete and perfect preparedness of 1914. The war machines of Europe were brought into collision in 1914 because they were so prepared as to make the postponement of war impossible.

I believe it is the war-machine of Japan which is today, in all the panoply of its preparedness, over-ruling the better judgment of the people of Japan and forcing the Japanese empire into that which is a war in fact if not in name.

The second, indeed, the first great purpose of preparedness is to enable a nation to wage war effectively and successfully, whether that war be offensive or defensive. The truth is that armaments, piled up to the very skies in the spirit of preparedness, do not guarantee either a successful defensive or an effective offensive. France and Belgium, in 1914, were ready, utterly and absolutely prepared for war. Yet there followed within a month of the beginning of the war, Germany's years of invasion and occupation of Belgium and France, despite the power of the armaments of the invaded and occupied lands. On the other hand, Germany's super-preparedness did not suffice to crown the offensive with victory. Preparedness did not make the German offensive triumphantly successful, nor yet the Belgian and the French defensive effective, until after years of most awful battle and blood-shed.

War preparedness does one thing more. It kills peace-preparedness. There can be no really effective peace-preparedness as long as it merely parallels without supplanting war-preparedness. The League of Nations is little more than a figment and a shadow, not so much because we are not included within the League, but because continuous and swollen war-preparedness nullifies it. The League of Nations is little more than a pious wish as long as the shadows of war-preparedness hang over it. *Rabbi Stephen S. Wise. Peace Programs. Dept. of Synagogue and Peace Extension. Cincinnati. n.d. p. 48-9.*

Now General Hagood, retired, is free to speak his mind about the way in which the army spends the taxpayer's money. His new book, *We Can Defend America,* gives his thesis in its title. General Hagood not only states that this country can be defended against any possible invasion (and by "this country" he means the stretch of territory which runs from Newfoundland to the Panama Canal on the Atlantic and from Alaska thru Hawaii to the Canal on the Pacific) but he declares (1) that it can be done easily; (2) that it can be done at far less cost than is at present being incurred by the war and navy departments; (3) that most of the money now being spent, and most of the training now being given the army and the air force, does not have in view defense of the United States at all but another expeditionary war to be carried on across the Atlantic or Pacific. Even the millions being spent on the air forces, General Hagood charges, have in view a bombing campaign to paralyze populations behind the fighting lines of a war being fought in Europe!

All these charges against the way in which the army, navy and air forces are spending their now-demanded *billion a year* will be bitterly controverted by the men who are spending the money, and by the subordinates who hope one day to know what it feels like to fling that much around. Nor do we assert that the case against such expenditures has been proved. It has, however, been raised. It has been raised in a sufficiently clear and plausible manner to demand honest and open examination. No issue as between pacifism and preparedness, defense and disarmament, is involved. This is a naked issue concerning the worth of the projects for which the army, the navy and the air forces say that they need to spend one billion dollars next year. Is the nation actually spending "millions for defense"? Or is it wasting millions at the behest of swivel-chair incompetents? Before Congress appropriates a dollar of the billion for which the President has asked there should be an open and searching investigation, devoted to determining for the first time the answers to these two questions: What are the nation's fighting services expected to do? Is this the way to do it? *Christian Century. F.* 10, '37. *p.* 177.

No elaborate proof is required to show that an arms race is not only a barometer of the danger of war but is also a cause of war. The financial burden of huge war machines presents the dilemma of bankruptcy or war. The world is now spending at the estimated rate of about $25,000 a minute, or $1,500,000 an hour. Revenues are eaten up by armament budgets as civil needs are sacrificed to military demands. Since ordinary revenues are not enough to satisfy the demands, the future is mortgaged in heavy loans. The fear of economic and social collapse is no doubt a restraining influence on foreign policy, but the economic strain is also a stimulus to strike before the load becomes unbearable and the arms become out-dated.

Armaments, however, are but one of a chain of causes leading to war. The race for arms is linked to economic, political, and spiritual factors of conflict. There is the struggle for markets, raw materials, and colonial advantages, and this economic conflict has been intensified by the depression. There is the desire for political prestige and power, backed by aggressive nationalism. There is the fear that derives from insecurity. It can be argued that a disarmament conference, which dealt with complex problems such as these, could get nowhere. And yet, can military questions be settled if they are divorced from the political and economic issues that underlie them? Is not the hidden reef on which previous attempts at arms limitation have been wrecked precisely this divorce of cause and effect?

The experience of the past surely indicates that a broader approach must be made to the problem of disarmament if it is to be solved successfully. The possibility of disarmament depends basically upon the degree of political, economic, and spiritual security which nations enjoy. Political security means the implementing of the principles of the Kellogg-Briand Pact with effective, non- military guarantees. Economic security involves the curbing of commercial rivalry through mutual trade concessions and economic cooperation. Spiritual security lies in the development of friendship and goodwill across all boundaries. Without the increase of this three-fold security among nations, there seems little hope for a genuine decrease in the perilous burden of armaments.

The world still faces the choice of peace or war, tho guns pile up, battle lines are formed, and armies already march on two continents. If the choice is to be peace, the peoples of the world must act, and act quickly, for the present drift means war. As Dr. Fosdick said in

a recent sermon, "Whether we like it or not, we are in
the position of mariners; we may decide to steer this
course or that, but if we decide to be undecided and drift,
then the ocean steps in and settles the matter." *World
Alliance for International Friendship Through the
Churches. News Letter. F. '38. p. 2.*

Why did great power—greater than we could ever
have again—fail in its function as a deterrent of aggression? Why did power fail to prevent war?

A dozen statesmen and historians have answered that
question, and all in the same way: The war could have
been prevented had Germany known beforehand that she
would have to meet the forces which she did finally meet.
Had she been able to foresee the resistance which her
policy would encounter, she would not have followed that
policy, and there would have been no war. This is
merely, of course, a concrete statement in terms of events
of an undeniable abstract truth. A party, person or nation can only be deterred by force from doing something
if he knows beforehand (a) what particular act will bring
the force into play, (b) believes that it will be brought
into play if he commits the act, and (c) that it will not
be brought into play if he refrains. (For if he believes
that he will incur the punishment anyhow, whether he
commits the crime or not, then, tho he knows that he will
incur the punishment, it will cease to have deterrent
effect.)

* * *

If we desire to make our power a means of preventing war, instead of being merely part of the means by
which we may win wars into which we "stagger and
blunder," we must make known beforehand the policy,
the status, the conditions whose maintenance we regard
as defence—for which we would fight.

If we merely say to the "have-not" states: "We own
a quarter of the world and propose to deny you any

rights of any kind in that area," then we shall get war, for the "have-not" states will take immense risks to alter those conditions.

If we say: "In the territory which is non-self-governing we will give you equal rights with ourselves; are prepared to have grievances investigated; are ready to develop as much as possible the principle of umpire, third-party judgment, to enlarge the organs of peaceful change; are prepared, further, to offer you the same principles of defence we claim for ourselves. We shall fight if needs be, not to maintain an empire closed against you, but to see that it is not conquered by you in order that you may close it against us; not for the status quo, but against change of the status quo by your force, on your sole decision; we shall fight, not for the purpose of being judge in our own cause—for we offer third-party judgment—but to see that you as the other litigant do not become the judge.

"For the defence of these principles we are ready to enter into alliance with all who stand by them, to form a defensive confederation based on the principle that an attack on one is an attack on all. It is open to you to join it when you are ready to abide by its conditions." If it becomes increasingly clear that our power is for the purpose of defending those conditions or principles, then it will make for peace. Otherwise, however great, it will not defend us and will not prevent war. *Sir Norman Angell. Nineteenth Century. Ag. '37. p. 141-2, 150-1.*

The Executive Committees of The Church Peace Union and the World Alliance for International Friendship through the Churches have adopted the following joint resolution on the May bill, H.R. 9604, now pending in the House of Representatives:

While approving any genuine measure to take the profits out of war, we strongly oppose the May bill, precisely because it does not insure the prevention of profiteering in time of

war.   It levies no tax whatever, and hence is incompatible
with its stated purpose.

On the other hand, it contains a number of measures
which involve serious dangers to our American system of
democratic government and to the liberties of the people.   It
threatens our traditional freedom thru the control of press
and radio.   It endangers the rights of those least able to bear
the burdens of war thru the control of labor.   It opens the
door to a military dictatorship.

We therefore earnestly petition the President and Congress
to withhold support from this bill.

Altho the ostensible purpose of the bill is "to prevent
profiteering in time of war and to equalize the burdens of
war," the one section dealing with war profits postpones
the creation of a law to tax away such profits.   The Secretary of the Treasury is to make "a continuing study . . .
from year to year" of taxation to "absorb all profits
above a fair normal return," and pass on his recommendations to Congress.   The May bill, in other words, provides neither a definition of war profits nor machinery to
tax them away.   It merely evades the problems by refer-
ring them to some future Congress.

The other ten sections of the bill have little to do
with profiteering but have much to do with the frame-
work for a military dictatorship, as envisaged in the Industrial Mobilization Plan.   The provisions are vague,
and dangerous for that very reason, since the broad
powers granted the executive are not limited by specific
guarantees for the protection of civil rights.   The indefinite clauses of the bill may be compared to blank
checks, upon which war-time boards could write in the
details of a military dictatorship.

Instead of equalizing the burdens of war, the May
bill could easily make for the greatest inequality by establishing military control over the common people on farm
and in factory.   The wedge for such control lies in the
provisions to conscript those between the ages of 21 and
31, to fix and alter prices for goods and "services," and to
control "industrial organizations" and "public services."

The rights of all citizens, moreover, are menaced by clauses affecting the press and radio. The wedge for control over the sources of information lies in the provisions to control public services, to license enterprises and to establish the priority of business orders. The press is excepted from the section on licenses, but control of newsprint and power would open the way for indirect dictation to the press.

It is interesting to note that the Japanese Diet has been resisting, despite war conditions and the pressure of the military, a bill to control industry and the press. The May bill bears certain similarities to the Japanese bill in that both open the way for dictatorial control by executive decree. Both bills point in the direction of the Nazi charter of 1933. But the May bill is offered to a democratic people in time of peace.

The May bill is the Trojan horse of militarism that certain groups are trying to bring within the gates of democracy. *World Alliance for International Friendship Through the Churches. News Letter. Mr. '38. p. 1.*

Vigorous protests are arising all over the world against the unprecedented rearmament of the nations. The judgment of the late Lord Grey of England that the World war was the result of the armament race early in the century is being quoted again and again. War is the inevitable result of excessive armaments and does not bring peace.

Warnings are being uttered on many sides that if this rearmament is not abandoned economic disaster as well as military disaster will follow. The National City Bank of New York, in its Bulletin of March 1937, deals at length with the economic results of this armament expenditure. It states that Great Britain expects to spend $1,500,000,000 annually for naval and military purposes in the next five years, which is four times the amount spent in 1913, and three times as much as the budget figures of three years ago. The French Chamber of Deputies has just approved a loan of $890,000,000 largely for military roads, industrial mobilization, and the strengthening of the concrete and steel fortresses. This is in addition to the regular national defense budget of the same amount.

This financial journal says that economically the above procedure is very unwholesome and undesirable in world affairs. It quotes the French Premier as saying, "It would be impossible to restrict the present armament race without provoking the danger of grave internal crisis." Business and labor seems to think that this demand coming to industry is a boon, but it means anything but real prosperity. It is a profligate and disastrous expenditure of capital, labor and credit in an unproductive way which produces derangements of trade relations, colossal debts, and ultimately the deadly influence of inflation will be felt in the business life of all countries. . . .

Much of the tension underlying the general expansion of armaments and the drift toward war has its foundation in economic and industrial conditions and especially in the breakdown of normal trading relations between the peoples of the world. The general economic crisis has led to a feverish search for economic self-sufficiency which finds its counterpart in the rapid growth of national armaments and the development of a psychology of conflict which, unchanged, must sooner or later result in war . . . In these circumstances, it would seem that there can be no political stability and no agreement to stop the competition in armaments without some substantial movement toward the mitigation of the distress arising out of economic and industrial circumstances.

So states a petition signed by four hundred well known British Liberals recently presented to the Prime Minister. The petition goes on to affirm that Great Britain, the greatest of all the trading powers, ought to make an immediate declaration as to the part she is prepared to play in adjusting these economic difficulties. The Memorial asks the government to announce to all countries, Great Britain's intention:

a. To do all in its power to expedite the proposed investigation under the League of Nations into the question of access to raw materials and to take such action as is necessary to carry out the conclusions reached.

b. To undertake a revision of the Ottawa agreements, such revision having as its minimum objective the creation of a low-tariff group which all other countries would be invited to join on a reciprocal basis.

c. To seek simultaneously with any group of nations outside the British Empire an agreement for the removal of quotas and the lowering of tariffs by a substantial percentage of their present amount.

d. To return to a policy of the Open Door for trade in all dependent territories under its control.

e. To present and advocate to other colonial powers concrete proposals for the general application of a strengthened mandate system under the League of Nations to all dependent territories not immediately ripe for self-government.

The process of building the world community must not be abandoned. Here in America at the present time in emphasizing the importance of keeping the United States out of war we are in a measure losing sight of the fact that the best way to keep our country out of war is to prevent war breaking out at any point in the world. This does not mean that we are to plunge into every international quarrel, but with our ships sailing the seven seas, our commerce circling the globe, our motion pictures being shown in every land, our automobiles driving over every road, our inventions in all modern art and science and industry being utilized to such an extent that they are transforming the customs and manners of the people in every land, we are not in a position to withdraw completely from the responsibilities of the world. War results from just such over-emphasis upon national needs and the interests of "safety first" as we see developing here at home.

Let us make our position clear—as follows:

1. We want no war either at home or abroad.

2. As citizens of the United States we will do everything possible to keep our country out of war.

3. As churchmen and women, we will put ourselves on record that while we stand ready to defend the soil of our land against invasion, we will have nothing to do with a war outside our own border.

4. Having gone thus far, let us use all our influence to see that the United States is represented at every congress, every convention, every conference which seeks to adjust the difficulties in which other nations find themselves. *World Alliance for International Friendship Through The Churches. News Letter. Ap. '37. p. 1-3.*

THE HANDBOOK SERIES

This series includes a number of subjects on public questions on which every man and woman should be well informed. The reprints are grouped (for convenience) according to the stand taken by the speaker quoted on the subject and an extensive bibliography guides one to further reading.

SERIES II

Cloth. Price $2.40 each. $12 for the Series of 6 in one order.

SERIES III